THAILAND
The MONOCLE Handbook

MONOCLE

First published in the United Kingdom in 2026 by
Monocle, Midori House, 1 Dorset Street,
London W1U 4EG
monocle.com
and Thames & Hudson Ltd,
6-24 Britannia Street, London WC1X 9JD
thamesandhudson.com

First published in the United States of America in 2026
by Monocle, Midori House, 1 Dorset Street,
London W1U 4EG
monocle.com
and Thames & Hudson Inc, 500 Fifth Avenue,
New York, New York 10110
thamesandhudsonusa.com

Monocle is a trading name of Winkontent Limited.
© 2026 Winkontent Limited

EU Authorised Representative: Interart S.A.R.L.
19 Rue Charles Auray, 93500 Pantin, Paris, France
productsafety@thameshudson.co.uk
interart.fr

British Library Cataloguing-in-Publication Data
A catalogue record for this book is available from
The British Library
Library of Congress Control Number: 2025947807

Edited by *James Chambers*

Designed by Monocle
Typeset in *Plantin*

Printed in Italy by *Graphicom*
ISBN 978-0-500-96650-1
01

Cover images
Front cover (clockwise)
Indra Regent Hotel by Foto Momo; The Decorum and
Tu Kab Khao by Natthawut Taeja
Back cover (clockwise from top left)
Andaz Hotel, Earth & Fire Ceramics and The Barai by
Natthawut Taeja; football on the beach by Joe Perri

Thailand

The MONOCLE Handbook

DISCOVER THAILAND

PART 01

We travelled the length and breadth of the mainland and traversed islands and mountains to scope out the best that this special Southeast Asian nation has to offer. Visit tea houses and modern restaurants; practitioners reinterpreting Thailand's traditional crafts; and the best places to recline in some of the country's most coveted hotels. *Sawasdee!*

PUT DOWN ROOTS

PART 02

Fallen in love with Thailand? Perhaps it's time to extend your stay – maybe indefinitely.
In this chapter we show you the best places to open a business, introduce you to the
architects and designers who can help turn your dream into a reality and peek inside
some Thai homes along the way. We also hear from bold entrepreneurs who have already
made the move.

ADDRESS BOOK

PART 03

Use this handy guide to help you plan your next trip. Here we present a full list of our
favourite places to stay, eat, shop and visit, organised by region. Whether you're heading
to Khon Kaen or Koh Samui we've got you covered.

Whether you're visiting for a city break, plotting a grand tour
or hoping to put down roots, *Thailand: The Monocle Handbook*
is your perfect travel companion. First off, here's a warm
welcome from our Bangkok-based Asia editor.

INTRODUCTION

JAMES CHAMBERS
Asia editor, Monocle

Thailand is what holiday dreams are made of. The fabulous street food, aromatic rice fields and coasts lined with palm trees have justifiably become famous across the globe and helped the Southeast Asian country to become a coveted destination.

Backpackers in the 1960s and 1970s popularised its once secret coves, hilltop retreats and fabled sunsets among foreigners. Books such as Alex Garland's *The Beach* and the James Bond film *The Man with the Golden Gun* also added to the mythology. But the country has changed in recent decades. Today its capital, Bangkok, rivals New York when it comes to the best in hospitality. And there are beach and rural escapes to suit any traveller. Everyone is welcome – that's a big part of the allure.

Thailand now offers not just breathtaking scenery and historic temples but also contemporary art, clever cocktails and world-class wellness retreats. Young creatives in Bangkok and Chiang Mai weave the craft traditions of the Karen people, the Hmong and other northern hill tribes into colourful new designs, while chefs from Isan cook up fresh takes on classic Thai dishes. It's a remarkable country that deserves to be explored: easy to get along with, easy to get to know and easy to love.

Helping you to experience the best of a nation is the point of every *Handbook* and there's plenty to discover in Thailand. This is why we chose it to be the subject of the sixth title in the series and the first destination outside Europe. Monocle has had a correspondent on the ground in Bangkok from the start and today it's one of our editorial bases in Asia – so if you're interested in a permanent relocation, we have some wise advice for you too.

Pop this sun-drenched book on your coffee table and start dreaming up your Thai adventure.

MAPS

Thailand's 76 provinces and its capital, Bangkok, share a proud history free of colonisation. Achieving this in Southeast Asia, once a playground for foreign powers, has taken deft diplomacy, a friendly demeanour and a flexible approach to borders.

At the end of the 19th century, the country was known as Siam and armies from Britain and France threatened it from east and west. King Chulalongkorn (Rama V for short) gradually annexed the northern state of Chiang Mai and oversaw a period of modernisation and nation-building that ultimately led in 1939 to the unifying name of Thailand for this Buddhist country.

The modern kingdom's landmass is similar to that of Spain. Its tourism backbone extends from the northern hills of Chiang Mai near Myanmar to the southern beaches of Phuket island in the Andaman Sea. The capital sits roughly at the centre of the map and it's even more central in the minds of its residents. Pretty much everywhere else is treated as "up country" to Bangkokians, who like to holiday within two-hours of the capital. But as this guide demonstrates, Thailand has something extraordinary to offer for locals and visitors in the capital and every one of its five distinct and culturally diverse regions.

Bangkok: Thailand's capital since 1782 drives commerce, culture and politics.

Central: The rice-bowl region home to the Chao Phraya river and Ayutthaya.

North: A misty and mountainous area, home to Chiang Mai and the "golden triangle" where the borders of Myanmar, Laos and Thailand converge.

Northeast: The country's northeastern hinterland bordered by the Mekong river, rich in national parks and wildlife.

East: Cruise boats enjoy the calm waters around eastern islands such as Koh Kut, Koh Samet, Koh Chang and Koh Mak.

South: The west coast lays claim to the country's most spectacular beaches, marine parks and spiciest cuisine.

EASTERN ISLANDS

SOUTHERN ISLANDS

NEED TO KNOW

Here we explain some of Thailand's unique traditions and quirks, from the nation's welcoming, relaxed nature, enthusiastic approach to festivals and insistence on the use of nicknames to its obsession with convenience stores and reverence for its royal family.

GREETINGS AND GESTURES
Say hello, wave goodbye

Thailand may be famous for being the land of smiles, but other everyday gestures are arguably more significant and respectful. First and foremost, the *wai*. Thais put their hands together in a prayer shape to say hello or thank you. The younger or less senior person will often raise their hands higher to their forehead, but such shows of deference are less important in modern life than making the gesture itself. A greeting *wai* is accompanied with a "*sawasdee ka*" (for women) or "*sawasdee krub*" (for men). To express gratitude, say "*khop khun ka*" or "*khop khun krub*". Attempts at speaking the language are warmly received but Thais have patience for translation apps. Return their good grace by remaining calm and unconfrontational. Thais will not step over someone, so be mindful of your outstretched legs – and certainly don't use your fingers or toes to point, as that is considered rude.

NICKNAMES
The long and short of it

Thai surnames are routinely long, frequently involve at least four syllables and the proper pronunciation of the English transliteration often misses out several silent letters. The widely accepted practice is to use first names instead and this applies to addressing everyone from the prime minister down, both verbally and in writing. The prefix *khun* – a gender-neutral equivalent of *san* in Japan – is placed at the front of a person's first name, or better yet, their nickname, which is normally chosen by their parents, friends or themselves. Some of the people featured in this book are better known as Banky, Dew, Golf, Sun, Sea, Pop, Champ, Jeab or Note.

CELEBRATIONS & FESTIVITIES
Party people

Being predominantly Buddhist does not stop the country showing fervour for other religious celebrations and cultural rituals, including Halloween and Chinese New Year. Christmas is particularly big in Thailand and festive decorations can often be spotted throughout the year in cafés, shops, hospitals and other workplaces. When it comes to Buddhist holidays, the mood turns a lot more sombre and sober. For a country synonymous with sun, fun and a fair bit of debauchery, Thailand can be very strict when it comes to drinking. Draconian legislation banning alcohol sales on Buddhist holy days is gradually easing, especially in tourist areas, but at times a beer can still be hard to come by.

CONVENIENCE STORES
The bare necessities

Thailand has one of the largest networks of 7-Elevens outside Japan (which has double the population), and the number continues to rise. These convenience stores are the place to buy bread, milk and instant noodles, as well as a Sim card, some stationery and one of the many energy drinks that keep the country's truck drivers and delivery workers running. Other essentials include the nasal inhalers that many sniff throughout the day to cure a litany of ailments. When looking for a flat, forget about proximity to supermarkets, shopping malls and schools; living in Thailand for any stretch of time means being within walking distance of a 7-Eleven.

A LAID-BACK SPIRIT
Easy does it

Buddhism is the most-followed religion and its beliefs and tenets permeate the country far beyond the ornate temples and monks in saffron-coloured robes. Society has a high degree of acceptance for different ways of life and this tolerance is at odds with many laws in outdated statute books. There is also a sense of fatalism for extreme events. The result is a nationwide zenness that covers political turmoil all the way down to Bangkok's often horrendous traffic. Daily happiness, family and a full stomach all trump making money, so don't be surprised to encounter businesses closed at lunchtime or laid-back shopkeepers seemingly ambivalent about closing a sale. Thailand is also a land of massages and wellness. The secret to being content is to treat this carefree spirit as gospel and learn how to say *"mai pen rai"* – a common reply that's the equivalent of "no worries".

TRANSPORT
Charting a course

There are many ways of getting around. Planes, trains, automobiles and buses, certainly, but also canal taxis, ferry boats, rice barges, motorbikes, tuk-tuks and elevated walkways. In Bangkok, the BTS Skytrain began operating in 1999. This extensive network – by Southeast Asian standards – has raised the capital above its traffic-clogged regional rivals. Jams still snarl parts of the city but modernisation is coming down the line. High-speed trains will one day run from Bangkok's new central station in Bang Sue to southern China via Laos. They may even run to Malaysia and Singapore. On the road, the pick-up truck is Thailand's unofficial national car – a fitting symbol for an automotive manufacturing hub known as the Detroit of Southeast Asia. Such is the domestic market for these flexible utility vehicles that dealerships put the newest model on a literal pedestal at the front of the forecourt.

THE ROYAL FAMILY
Stand on ceremony

The monarchy is part of the fabric of Thai society in very visible ways. The top universities are named after previous kings from the reigning Chakri dynasty, as are Bangkok's main roads. Large portraits of the current king, Vajiralongkorn – commonly known as Rama X – are displayed inside offices, on highways and even on the façades of tall buildings. Each day has its own colour and every Thai will know their birth colour. Rama X was born on a Monday, so civil servants wear yellow polo shirts on the first day of the week. The king's anthem (distinct from the national anthem sounded in parks, on TV and on national radio at 08.00 and 18.00 every day) is played at the cinema before each screening.

PART 01

DISCOVER THAILAND

Take a tour of the country's best hospitality,
design, culture and architecture – plus the beaches
and outdoor spaces not to be missed.

Whether you're travelling for business or pleasure, for a long weekend of cultural pursuits and fine dining, or an extended stay connected to nature, here's our guide to the best places to stay in Thailand.

WHERE TO STAY

As one of Southeast Asia's most visited destinations, it's no surprise that Thailand has a place to stay for every possible taste and preference. Whether you're looking for a sophisticated urban bolthole offering an all-amenities experience in the heart of bustling Bangkok, or a sanctuary by the beach or in the mountains that brims with nature's tropical offerings to distract you, Thailand has it all. The country's hotels are also a great place to experience local culture. Many boast exceptional restaurants showcasing regional cuisine and shops selling the highest quality handmade ceramics, homewares and textiles. However, the crowning glory of a stay at a Thai hotel is the gentle, easy-going hospitality that makes you feel relaxed and right at home no matter where you started your journey. To help navigate the multitude of options, we've gathered our favourite places to lay down our heads, from luxurious, ultra-private estates to switch-off-from-it-all beachfront retreats.

THE EDIT

1 **Urban hotels**
From Bangkok to Chiang Mai and cutting-edge architecture to superbly renovated historic gems, these are our top picks for city stays.

2 **Coastal hotels**
Thailand's coastline glistens with polished upscale outposts and palm-thatched guesthouses. Here are some of our favourite sea-lapped spots.

3 **Rural hotels**
A selection of countryside boltholes that celebrate Thailand's tropical greenery and impressive terrain.

4 **The experts**
Three hospitality insiders give us their thoughts on the present and future of the country's hotel industry.

For bookings, see pages 216—218.

URBAN HOTEL
THE SUKHOTHAI
Bangkok

With a name meaning "the dawn of happiness" in Sanskrit, The Sukhothai – with its beautiful courtyard, lotus ponds, hushed pavilions and well-kept gardens – is a bubble of serenity amid the downtown chaos. There's an old-world quality here: red-brick *chedi*s (Buddhist monuments) and ancient Khmer-inspired carvings feature heavily, along with live *khim* music (a traditional stringed instrument) in the evenings and at weekends. Guest rooms, meanwhile, keep things up-to-date with polished teak, bronze, silks by Jim Thompson and handmade stoneware ceramics. The Club Wing offers an open bar and a lounge with views of the city.

Exercise in serenity
Celadon, the hotel's restaurant, serves a Thai menu. If you want a way to burn off any excess calories after your meal, try the hotel's 25-metre pool – or if you prefer to pound the pavement, nearby Lumphini Park is great for a run.

015

URBAN HOTEL
ROSEWOOD
Bangkok

URBAN HOTEL
PUBLIC HOUSE
Bangkok

A colourful mural by Spanish-Mexican artist Rafael Uriegas sets the tone at this lively independent hotel. The 79-key corner site is close to some of Bangkok's best drinking and dining options – including Appia (*see page 53*) and Alone Together (*see page 86*) – and also provides workspaces for meetings. The owners, husband and wife Paul and Angie Sachdev, have come to hospitality from careers in fashion retail and combine welcoming interiors with subtly attentive service and a splash of fun. "Over the years we have stayed everywhere from budget hotels to five-star luxury," says Paul. "We found we preferred boutique hotels and noticed the gap in the Thai market."

Rosewood Bangkok occupies an arresting KPF-designed structure whose form is an abstract representation of the *wai*, the Thai greeting gesture. The two high-rises, linked by recessed terraces, rise 30 floors to create a striking statement. In keeping with the hotel group's preference for residential-style interiors, this outpost employs plush furnishings, brass accents and marble bathrooms, as well as glass walls to allow natural light. The Gallery showcases Thai artists, supplying further personality. At Lakorn, guests sample dishes from across Thailand, and Nan Bei deals in regional Chinese cuisine. It would be remiss to not cap off an evening at Lennon's, where you'll find a selection of innovative, music-inspired cocktails.

URBAN HOTEL
MANDARIN ORIENTAL
Bangkok

Thailand's oldest international hotel dates back nearly 150 years and patrons old and new come to this riverside address to experience the country's famed hospitality. Almost 1,000 passionate, impeccably dressed staff turn out in uniform to cater to guests' needs, from the room butlers to the experienced restaurant managers at The Verandah and Lord Jim. Visitors are greeted by liveried "hotel ambassadors" wearing traditional silk trousers and a long-sleeved "raj pattern" shirt tied with a silk wrap. A green-and-gold pointed helmet completes the look. The Verandah overlooking the busy Chao Phraya river is a good spot for lunch during the cooler months, while The Bamboo Bar always has a special atmosphere.

URBAN HOTEL
NA TANAO 1969
Bangkok

Run by Jitrapat "Name" Israngkura Na Ayudhya, this Bangkok "hometel" is rich with family history and once contained the entrance to Name's grandmother's house before becoming the plot of the hotel. Ancestral relics, including his mother's sewing machine and father's violin, can be found throughout and rooms are lovingly dedicated to family members, all fitted into a slender townhouse just 3.5 metres wide. Designed by Patchara + Ornnicha Architecture, an innovative ventilation system keeps the building light and airy and the open spaces – including the coffee shop and living room-cum-wine bar – serve as communal hubs. "We would like guests to experience local Thai living," says Name.

URBAN HOTEL
THE SIAM
Bangkok

This five-star stay on the Chao Phraya river is proudly owned and operated by a Thai family. The Sukosols opened The Siam in 2012 and worked with designer Bill Bensley to capture the charm of Bangkok from a century ago. The antique furniture and lighting come from the collection of Krissada Sukosol Clapp, a Thai singer and actor who calls his creation a "museum mansion home". The restaurant makes use of stilt houses, while other nods to the country's heritage include a Thai boxing ring and a studio for buddhist Sak Yant ink tattoos. "I named our hotel 'The Siam', so I had to do it justice," says Clapp. Privacy comes with having just 38 keys – and every guest gets butler service.

URBAN HOTEL
CAPELLA BANGKOK
Bangkok

Capella Bangkok has one of the most coveted locations in the city – each guest pad has a balcony featuring an unobstructed view of the Chao Phraya river. The result is that the water remains a focal point throughout your stay. To further emphasise the expansive vistas, the rooms and suites have a relaxing vibe thanks to a medley of whites, greys and blondewood, while the villas have private gardens. A Himalayan salt scrub treatment followed by a visit to the Tea Lounge makes for the perfect lazy afternoon. Afterwards, dine at riverside restaurant Phra Nakhon, or book a table at the two-Michelin-starred Côte by Mauro Colagreco, for its menu influenced by French and Italian cuisine.

URBAN HOTEL
GRAND HYATT ERAWAN BANGKOK
Bangkok

There are few spots better tailored to Bangkok's business community than the Grand Hyatt Erawan Bangkok. Set in the capital's Ratchaprasong precinct, the hotel sits on the doorstep of several major retail destinations and is linked to the wider city via the BTS network. The I.Sawan gym and spa provide travellers with the ultimate jet-lag cure but to maximise rest check into one of the signature Garden Villas. Among verdant gardens on the building's fifth floor, these suites prioritise seclusion with their private terraces perched high above the city. Guests can also swing by the Erawan Bakery for a pastry or book a table at the Erawan Tea Room for afternoon tea with views of the neighbouring Erawan Shrine.

URBAN HOTEL
BAAN POMPHET
Ayutthaya

Saralee Rattanapuchpong hired Bangkok studio Onion (*see page 192*) to design her eight-key hotel and restaurant. Rather charmingly, the waterfront property includes nods to river prawns, a local delicacy, as seen in the lampshades made from *chanang* fishing traps – her family operates a river-prawn restaurant, Ban U Tong, on the same road. *Baan* means "house" or "home" in Thai and the hotel gets the second half of its name and additional design cues from the nearby ruins of a brick fortress known as Pom Phet. The bricks deployed in the property are of a locally sourced variety produced in a special size and a distinctive orange hue. Guests and diners can all enjoy the same calming view of the river and its daily, slow-moving traffic – a mix of floating water hyacinth, tour boats circling the old town and barges transporting rice and other goods between north and south. "The daybeds outside each room are my favourite space because you can watch the river and the leaves of the Bodhi tree swaying in the wind," says Rattanapuchpong.

RURAL HOTEL
Z9 RESORT
Kanchanaburi

Guests at Z9 get their first glimpse of the resort when they negotiate an S-bend in the road and see a reservoir and mountain range in the distance. Sarawoot Jansaeng-Aram of architecture firm Dersyn Studio has framed how guests visually interact with the hotel's setting on Srinagarindra Lake upon arrival. "We wanted the curvy, wave shape of the villas to match the mountain range in the distance, so we used a natural-stone-looking finish on the roof to help it blend into the surrounding nature," says Jansaeng-Aram, who also used leftover wood from the old hotel that stood on the site to decorate the rooms.

Shore thing
Z9's lake location makes the water a constant feature. Facilities include a private pontoon for swimming and kayaking, while the waterfalls of Sai Yok and Erawan national parks are nearby. Several villas have been added since the hotel was completed in 2019, including Pla2, a standalone example for eight. Hidden from sight around the headland, it is only accessible by boat.

COASTAL HOTEL
THE BARAI
Hua Hin

To step onto the grounds of The Barai is to enter a sanctum of health and wellbeing. At the heart of the hotel property – accessed via a subtly-lit entry sequence – is the spa. Finished in ochre and burgundy tones, this maze of 18 treatment rooms is complete with soaking pools, rain showers and steam rooms, and is centred around a revitalising programme of personalised wellness treatments. The eight exclusive suites are equally impressive. Sitting on almost 2 hectares (4.5 acres) of beachfront, the guest rooms boast private plunge pools, tailored butler service and pristine views of the Gulf of Thailand.

Spa light
Designed by Thai architect Lek Mathar Bunnag, The Barai is defined by a clever interplay of water and light, taking inspiration from Cambodia's ancient Khmer *baray*s (reservoirs) that are thought to be sacred and healing.

COASTAL HOTEL
CHIVA-SOM
Hua Hin

Set on a lush, tropical beach in Hua Hin – known as the Hamptons of Thailand – Chiva-Som was one of the country's first wellness resorts when it opened in 1995. Since then, it has been a top destination for those looking to relax and reset. The offerings include fitness programmes, treatments (a papaya body wrap does wonders to soften the senses) and organic fare using produce often grown on site – the detoxing sorbets lend a degree of indulgence to healthy eating. Of the 54 teak and bamboo-decorated guest rooms and suites, the Leelawadee Suite is the standout – it has a private garden and is ideal for longer stays, allowing ample time to root out any leftover tension with a Thai boxing class.

COASTAL HOTEL
THE STANDARD
Hua Hin

An easy-going tropical breeze hits as soon as you set foot on the grounds of The Standard's Hua Hin outpost. From the towering rain trees at the entrance to the handsome decor reminiscent of the mid-century style, the hotel is a touch of paradise in this seaside town, once a quiet fishing village and now a coastal haven for locals and tourists. The Hyatt-owned group's signature use of rich, retro colours (splashes of sunshine yellow appear throughout the 196 rooms, suites and villas) is enhanced by the bright backdrop of the beach. "It's effortlessly cool in an unexpected place," says Amar Lalvani, president and creative director of Hyatt Corporation's lifestyle division. "My favourite thing is the landscape and how the hotel interacts with it." When in need of refuelling after an afternoon by the pool, sample the superb selection of drinking and dining options: Lido is a relaxed all-day spot; The Juice Café is known for its cold-pressed blends; and Praça (see page 59) is the signature restaurant set in a restored heritage house with sweeping views of the shore.

URBAN HOTEL
137 PILLARS
Chiang Mai

At the centre of this all-suite property is a remarkable teak house supported by 137 pillars. Built as the head-quarters of a British trading company in 1889, the house was renovated in the early 2000s. Today, lush planting (including a 150-year-old rubber tree), reflection ponds, a swimming pool and a croquet lawn provide the perfect counterpoint to the lively local neighbourhood. Guests are housed in two-storey contemporary suites with teak detailing and each with its own outdoor living space. General manager, Anne Arrowsmith, describes the ambience as "elegance with an absence of arrogance" and represents the hotel's commitment to personal hospitality by regularly being found greeting guests on arrival.

RURAL HOTEL
RAYA HERITAGE
Chiang Mai

Raya Heritage is an example of the magic that happens when contemporary design meets centuries-old traditional knowledge. Guiding the project from the purchase of the land to the opening of the 38-suite hotel in 2018, general manager, Naphat Nutsati, says that it "makes the hotel not just a place to stay but a living showcase of northern Thailand's artisanal heritage". For two years prior to opening, the design team worked closely with artisans across the region. Their handcrafted furniture, decorative artifacts and accessories were incorporated into the resort's design, perfectly complementing the contemporary architecture by Boonlert Hemvijitraphan.

Design of the times
Every detail of Raya Heritage – from the architecture to furniture, textiles and incidental objects – is designed to connect with the local Lan Na culture, providing a historical link to the 13th-century Lan Na kingdom that included parts of modern-day Myanmar, Laos, China and Thailand.

URBAN HOTEL
TAMARIND VILLAGE
Chiang Mai

RURAL HOTEL
TATVANI ESTATE
Chiang Rai

Guests enter Tamarind Village – which is named for the 200-year-old tree in the courtyard – via a bamboo-lined driveway. The natural canopy creates a sense of calm and peace that permeates the rest of the property. Architect Ong-ard Satrabhandhu based the layout on a traditional northern Thai temple, with long corridors providing multiple entrances and exits. Colourful fabrics produced by artisans from the Hmong and Karen hill tribes that surround Chiang Mai add comfort. "When we took over this property more than 20 years ago, we wanted to uplift the standards of hospitality in Chiang Mai and promote more upscale tourism," says Tipchaya "Rin" Phongsathorn, CEO of Premier Hotels & Resorts.

As a one-key, 11.7-hectare private estate with room for 18 guests, Tatvani is not a hotel in the conventional sense. Accommodation is distributed across six villas, each named after a variety of koi (they're bred on the grounds). The all-inclusive experience includes drinking and dining, spa treatments, hiking excursions, Thai cooking classes and visits to the Tatvani elephant sanctuary, where the gentle giants are looked after by custodians of the Karen hill tribe. Staff are on hand when you need them and will leave you to your relaxation when you don't. "Tatvani is a family," says estate manager John Dunbar. "Everyone who works here is committed not just to the estate but the wider community and the natural landscape."

URBAN HOTEL
AD LIB
Khon Kaen

Ad Lib hotel is the crowning glory of the 28-storey Khon Kaen Innovation Center in Thailand's northeastern Isan region. "I didn't want there to be any incongruent design," says Tak Sriratanobhas, the building's general manager. "Every choice had to be woven into the theme – and Isan culture is the theme." The unabashedly sleek modern hotel offers a rooftop pool, live music venue and two restaurants, including an east-facing breakfast room that greets the rising sun. From 23 floors up, the city sparkles brilliantly below. "This hotel is not just for tourists," says Sriratanobhas. "I want locals to see their culture reflected here, too." The region is known for its textiles and a woven Isan motif sets the aesthetic tone for every room.

RURAL HOTEL
SALA
Khao Yai

Bangkok families regularly head to Khao Yai – Thailand's first national park and uncharted territory for most foreign tourists – for the fresh air, slightly cooler temperatures and stunning mountain views. Sala's Khao Yai destination delivers on this and then some. Guests of the boutique chain get to stay in standalone villas with private swimming pools, individual gardens and uninterrupted views of the surrounding hillsides. "It's small, it's private and it sits right in the middle of nature," says Dick Simarro, vice president of Sala Hospitality Group. "You wake up to these incredible views of the hills and vineyards."

Class Onion
Bangkok-based studio Onion (*see page 192*) designed this hotel in 2009. A later second phase added a few more villas and an infinity pool that extends out towards the horizon and seemingly floats above the valley below. Large gatherings of families and friends looking for a lofty home away from home can book the three-bedroom villa with rooftop pool.

COASTAL HOTEL
MASON
Pattaya

COASTAL HOTEL
ANDAZ HOTEL
Pattaya

This beach retreat is a bubble of calm outside Pattaya City. "Our vision for the hotel was always to do justice to what was pre-existing – this wonderful, undulating topography," says general manager Ranjeet Rajebhosale. At the centre is the "Village Square", an open horseshoe plot that includes Wok Wok, specialising in Thai comfort dishes; La Cucina, a lively Italian spot; and Village Butcher, a classic steakhouse. The 18 variants of rooms range from stunning 50 sq m dwellings with balconies and garden views, up to a three-bedroom heritage house. Walk down to the shore for the Fish Club restaurant, order tuna steak tacos and a bottle of Andaz IPA, then watch while the sun sinks to the horizon.

Mason in the south of Pattaya is a hidden gem. It offers ultra-modern private villas with panoramic views of the Gulf of Thailand in a beachy, cultural enclave that is home to a community of contemporary artisans, many of whom have left the bustle of Bangkok behind. Each of the 35 individual villas is an architectural statement: the exposed concrete structures feature floor-to-ceiling glass, neutral expanses of polished stone and fine textiles, contrasted with light wood accents. "It's design-focused; we're appealing to people who want a taste of luxury," says Pornpun Ratanapitakkul, Mason's general manager. "We have a lot of repeat customers who love our villas and the world we've created."

COASTAL HOTEL
THE DEWA KOH CHANG
Koh Chang

Offering expansive views of the Gulf of Thailand, The Dewa still maintains the sense of privacy expected of a premium island bolthole. Close enough to Bangkok for a long weekend getaway, being just an hour's flight away from the country's bustling capital, The Dewa sits beachside on Koh Chang – one of the most southeastern Thai islands in the gulf. Having opened in 2007 as a 59-key resort, its stone walkways lead guests from their rooms towards the white sand beach and panoramic views of the temptingly clear blue waters. Dotted along the route, stop-offs at The Restaurant and The Café promise light bites after lazy hours spent in the sun.

Tall and tropical
Among the first to embrace what is now widely appreciated as the "tropical rustic" aesthetic, The Dewa's architecture departs from the typically modest, low-rise buildings found across eastern Thailand. The venue is characterised by exposed concrete walls and double-height timber ceilings supported by towering columns, topped by thatched or shingled roofs.

COASTAL HOTEL
THE RETREAT
Koh Chang

A beautiful open-air lobby sits beneath the shade of a circular wooden roof at the entrance of this tropical, Zen-inspired 38-key beachfront hotel. This sets the tone for a host of other amenities, including an infinity pool with sun loungers set into its shallow reaches that promises peaceful, lazy days. Other five-star facilities have been given a similar feel – guests can indulge in a volcanic sand bath treatment at the spa or a harmonious fusion of Thai, Japanese and pan-Asian cuisines at the oceanfront Zojima restaurant. The artworks, cushion covers and baskets found in the hotel are made by local artisans, many of which can be purchased on request.

Time for teak
The Retreat makes extensive use of aged teak reclaimed by local carpenters from abandoned houses in northern Thailand. The wood has been made into elegantly contemporary beds, desks, flooring and sun loungers, resulting in a seamless design that preserves and interweaves heritage and architectural materiality into the fabric of the hotel.

COASTAL HOTEL
PARADEE
Koh Samet

Paradee resort, which gets its name from the Sanskrit word for paradise, is a title well-earned. With sunny yellow interiors and comforting nooks, all beautifully trimmed with hardwood, the quiet of each room encourages guests to take a seat, take stock and relax. Palm trees line the pathways between the 40 villas, scattering coins of light about your feet as the sun dapples through the greenery overhead. Towards the seafront, the resort's main dining area – with the no-nonsense name The Restaurant – is built in the distinctive circular design of a Thai *sala*: a familiar open pavilion designed to provide shade and act as a meeting point. Appearing as though among a camp of conical tents, a communal feel is emphasised, with views of the Gulf of Thailand available from Sunset Bar.

COASTAL HOTEL
KOH MUNNORK PRIVATE ISLAND
Koh Man Nok

EASTERN HOTELS | DISCOVER THAILAND

The same family has operated Koh Munnork for more than 30 years. A new generation is now in charge and the emphasis is on mindfulness and preserving the natural environment. "People interpret the island differently. Some want to rest, some to recover and some to reconnect," says creative director and head of operation Winchana Prucksananont, who has been coming here since he was a baby. The architecture graduate has led the resort's development while getting to know every inch of rock. "Nature is always fascinating. It doesn't have to be clear blue skies and turquoise waters," he says. "I find my peace being in the middle of the water."

A pierless experience
There is no pier on this private island in the Gulf of Thailand so every guest steps onto the sand from a small, shallow-bottomed boat. There are only 22 bungalows on the property, no televisions and barely any phone signal. Rooms have air-conditioning but electricity is shut off for several hours each morning and guests are encouraged to wake early to make the most of the sunlight.

COASTAL HOTEL
RAYAVADEE RESORT
Krabi

On the sharpest point of the curving Phranang Peninsula, Rayavadee Resort is a class apart, with coconut groves swaying in the breeze and a sweet coastal scent drifting along the pathways to the hotel's two-floor pavilions. In its three decades, this refuge has mastered the art of providing guests with choices. Should you desire a private sauna, there is a villa so equipped. If in need of a butler, a service can be offered for your stay. Should you prefer something quieter and closer than the ocean, there are leafy villas with private pools in the front garden. For those wishing to enjoy dinner on the beach, a sea-facing restaurant allows you to sit back with a drink, listen to the lapping of the waves and take it all in.

COASTAL HOTEL
THE SAROJIN
Khao Lak

It's difficult to resist this open, family-friendly resort dedicated to all things wellness. Since its establishment, massage therapists have waited on guests hand and foot – and worked neck and back – and the tropical idyll has found decades-long success in facilitating the slow life. Its storied history began with Lady Sarojin, the daughter of a Thai nobleman who became world famous for her hospitality towards guests of her parents. Today, she is the symbol and standard-bearer of the resort's mission, embodied in their premium offerings that include Ayurvedic treatments, body scrubs and facials. There are four boarding options available; the Garden Residence, the Jacuzzi Pool Suite and two different Pool Residences.

COASTAL HOTEL
DEVASOM KHAO LAK
Khao Lak

Everyone holidays differently. At Devasom – a portmanteau of the Sanskrit words *deva* (angel) and *ashram* (residence) – even the most indecisive traveller will want for nothing, thanks to a scenic horizon-edge pool, a Michelin-honoured meal, spa treatments and private cooking classes. In the village of Khao Lak, this 69-key hotel has easy access to the sea and a series of natural lagoons. A copse of coconut trees belonging to a plantation can be found nearby. For a dose of local culture, there's a shuttle bus that runs three times daily into the town centre. On return, try the wonderful Takola restaurant, where you'll find local southern Thai dishes such as *moo hong*, the popular curried crab with betel leaves, or the comforting *tom yum goong*. It all goes well with the sommeliers' creative pairings.

COASTAL HOTEL
GARRYA TONGSAI BAY SAMUI
Koh Samui

When Akorn Hoontrakul first set eyes on Tongsai Bay on the island of Koh Samui, he declared it was "love at first sight". Having bought the land just seven days later, the hotelier spent three months sleeping on the beach as he mapped out the island's first ever five-star hotel. The resort, which wraps around a generous private bay, is currently owned by his son and daughter-in-law. There is a clear commitment to sustainability – rather notably, 70 per cent of the land remains untouched. "Contemplative pockets" are scattered around the resort to encourage guests to completely immerse themselves in nature and the stripped-back approach to furnishing and decoration helps further this sense of purity and calm. "It's not just a destination – it's a feeling," says general manager Manuel Lang.

COASTAL HOTEL
CASTAWAY
Koh Lipe

Koh Lipe is in the Strait of Malacca close to Malaysia, and is one of Thailand's southernmost islands – making it much less tourist-heavy than similar locations. Castaway is in close proximity to the island's Walking Street, which is full of retail and restaurant options, yet the resort feels like a world apart, as it sits on the golden sands of Sunrise Beach. There's an easy-going spirit here, with accommodation in sophisticated darkwood bungalows topped with thatched roofs and elevated on sturdy foundational stilts to keep guests cool in the island's heat. Due to the intimate size of the islet, you have easy access to all that's on offer. Scuba diving is particularly popular due to the stunning coral reef nearby and instructors can be hired on site.

COASTAL HOTEL
THE SANCTUARY
Koh Phangan

Despite being a short boat trip from the Full Moon party frenzy that Koh Phangan is hailed for, The Sanctuary, set in the Chumphon archipelago on the pristine Haad Tien beach, is far removed from the carousing chaos. Here, guests discover a restorative combination of healthy smoothies, spa therapies, yoga retreats and detox programmes designed to enrich and revitalise. To maximise your rest, spend the night in the rustic Tree House sheltered by a banyan tree – or, better yet, stay in the Ocean View Villa for its thatched roof, open-plan terrace and unparalleled panoramic views. Cocooned between a coconut grove and hillside jungle, the grounds are truly idyllic.

COASTAL HOTEL
AKATSUKI
Koh Samui

Koh Samui is awash not only with five-star hotels, but also some remarkable private villas that offer absolute seclusion. Top among them is Villa Akatsuki, a sequestered stay on the island's west coast. Designed by Tokyo-based Riccardo Tossani Architecture, the six-bedroom retreat is a coherent blend of Thai and Japanese design. Wooden trusses hold up vaulted ceilings, creating a sense of height and space, and large slatted doors invite the tropical breeze inside. The private spa and infinity pool provide top-tier rejuvenation, while those looking to explore can enjoy an afternoon in a kayak or partake in a Muay Thai session on the lawn.

Relative calm
"Akatsuki was born from a deeply personal moment," says owner Eyal Armoni. Although originally intended to be a second home for Armoni's family, the property quickly became public. "I wish to share the beauty and serenity of the space with others and hope guests experience the same peace, privacy and connection to nature that my family cherishes," he adds.

COASTAL HOTEL
KAMALAYA
Koh Samui

"Kamalaya was born from the unique journey of its founders," says Gopal Kumar, the property's general manager and group director of wellness development. Dreamed up by a former monk and his partner – a doctor of traditional Chinese medicine – the holistic wellness retreat, clustered on a hillside parcel of land thick with vegetation, is a meeting point of eastern traditions and western practices. Guests can work on their fitness, sleep and gain emotional "resilience and balance" through tailored programmes. There's also an excellent roster of tai chi, yoga and *qi gong* classes. The land itself is said to have healing qualities and architect Robert Powell played into this by positioning the property around a centuries-old meditation cave that's tucked between winding streams and lotus ponds. He created a village-like quality, with villas dotted about the jungle, connected by stone bridges. The clever use of boulders – reimagined as shelving and decorative features that protrude into rooms – brings the outside in. An ambient backing track of birdsong helps lull you further.

COASTAL HOTEL
KOYAO BAY PAVILIONS
Koh Yao Noi

COASTAL HOTEL
PIMALAI RESORT & SPA
Koh Lanta

Koh Lanta has long been a closely kept secret among locals. That is until Anurat Tiyaphorn built the Pimalai Resort & Spa on a 40-hectare tropical plot, acquired when there were no roads or electricity supply on the island. The villas – distinctive for their hipped clay-tiled roofs – have since been blended into the terrain to avoid spoiling the greenery. "The design is meant to complement rather than compete with the surrounding landscape," says co-owner Charintip Tiyaphorn. Teak floors, bird-cage lampshades and a long-tail boat in the restaurant add to local flavour. Evenings here are remarkable: the Hillside Oceanview private pool villa directly faces the sunset and the private beach is best enjoyed on a twilight stroll.

Koyao Bay Pavilions may be off the beaten track but it will reward those with an intrepid spirit. Seemingly adrift in Phang Nga Bay, with Phuket across the strait to the west and Krabi to the east, Koh Yao Noi offers tropical gardens and abundant wildlife, with the hotel nestled on the island's shore. The three beach suites and eight villas, some with private pools, celebrate seclusion. If you take the short, easy saunter down to the nearby rice paddies, La Sala – a composed fusion restaurant with a largely Mediterranean-Thai menu – will be there to greet you. The grilled squid and sautéed garlic prawns pair harmoniously with produce from the on-site garden and a bottle of wine from the house cellar.

COASTAL HOTEL
SIX SENSES
Koh Yao Noi

The 56 villas of the Six Senses resort are cocooned in the shade of trees from a former rubber plantation and decked out with private pools, sunken bathtubs and alfresco dining areas that celebrate the surrounding natural environment. "Six Senses Yao Noi was born from a vision to let the island speak for itself," says general manager Graham Grant. Tasteful nods to Thai culture can be found in the hotel's use of vibrant *kolae* fishing boat colours, while moments of rest and indulgence are encouraged at the spa and in the three gourmet restaurants. "We invite our guests to live as the island does – naturally, beautifully and without hurry," Grant adds.

Sense of direction
This secluded island on Thailand's west coast won't be found on most travellers' itineraries. Planted between Phuket and Krabi, and free from the bustling footfall of tourists, Koh Yao Noi has long flown under the radar and promises an uninterrupted visit.

COASTAL HOTEL
AMANPURI
Phuket

Temple building
Amanpuri's temple-like structures, with their lyrical lines and pitched roofs, are the work of the American architect Ed Tuttle. The more recent addition of a floating roof pavilion by Kengo Kuma is a masterful combination of contemporary and traditional design.

Amanpuri, the first opening for the legendary Aman group, is a paean to the Buddhist architecture of Ayutthaya, the ancient capital of Siam. Coconut palms, expansive *salas* and secluded sun decks encourage outdoor living, while inside a refined medley of art, antiques, silk furnishings and teak fittings showcase local Thai craftsmanship. "The property's tranquil energy, connection to Thai culture and seamless integration with nature make it a destination like no other," says general manager Gearoid Lyons. Be sure to meander along the floating walkways to the holistic wellness centre for use of the saunas and outdoor Jacuzzi.

COASTAL HOTEL
TRISARA
Phuket

Trisara's 39 villas are positioned across a terraced hillside so that each one is shielded by old-growth greenery while simultaneously benefitting from clear views of the Andaman Sea. They keep watch over a 2km stretch of private coastline, so guests can amble down to the beach and take a dip in the lapping waves out front. They are also encouraged to take a stroll through the extensive grounds to Pru, Phuket's first Michelin-starred destination. "My family envisioned a place where guests could retreat into nature without sacrificing comfort," says Kittisak "Kitt" Pattamasaevi, CEO of Montara Hospitality Group. "Trisara is a space created not just for comfort but for deep, restorative rest."

COASTAL HOTEL
THE NAKA PHUKET
Phuket

Designed by Duangrit Bunnag Architect in 2012, The Naka Phuket's geometric glass and concrete villas overhang the mountainside, creating the illusion of floating rooms. The cantilever design is complemented by views from panoramic windows and the nearby reflective infinity pool ensures a clear line of sight down to the Andaman Sea. Inside, the attention to lines and angles continues: beds are aligned to face the shore and balconies are carefully positioned in sun-soaked spots. Only accessible from a winding mountain road, this modern retreat is kept off the beaten track deliberately, although Patong is a mere 6km away for those who want to venture into the town to sample its vibrant nightlife.

COASTAL HOTEL
ROSEWOOD
Phuket

Of Thailand's many island hotels, Rosewood Phuket is a standout. Days here are spent dozing on sundecks, being pampered at the Asaya spa and strolling on the shoreline of Emerald Bay. The main pool and its floating walkways are at the heart of the property and the ground-level, apartment-style Lagoon Pool pavilions are designed to feel premium yet homely. "Our job is to make you really slow down and unwind as completely as possible," says managing director Andrew Turner. It is also a culinary hotspot with a trio of dining options. We suggest Ta Khai – a Thai restaurant helmed by local chef couple Khun Nun and Khun Yai – for a spicy serving of *gaeng massaman nuea* (a premium beef-and-potato curry).

Thailand offers an incredible wealth of accommodation options, from rustic beachfront villas to some of the most feted hotels in the world. We speak to three people in the industry to find out about their professional journeys.

MEET THE EXPERTS

HOTELIER
SIRADEJ "CHAMP" DONAVANIK
Dusit Thani

Donavanik's grandmother was a Thai hospitality pioneer who opened the original Dusit Thani hotel in Bangkok.

What's your role at Dusit International?
I am heading our development efforts globally, basically growing our properties and brands throughout the world. Hospitality is in my blood.

What did your grandmother teach you?
We always like to overcomplicate things. People are the most important aspect of hospitality and that's true whether you're talking about the legacy of the past or the AI of the future.

How has the hotel landscape changed during your lifetime?
It's become far more competitive. Every single brand under the sun is here and there's a lot more coming in – both international and independent. Younger generations are starting to put their own mark on the industry and Bangkok now has quite a nice balance.

How does Bangkok compare to every other city you visit?
I call it organised chaos. Everything just works but it's very raw and rough around the edges. I've been to some crazy bars on Sukhumvit 24 where they serve wine on tap and people are dancing on the tables. Bangkok is a mecca for consumers.

HOTELIER
ANCHALIKA KIJKANAKORN
Akaryn Hotel Group

Kijkanakorn left her finance career in London in 2001 to convert her parents' beach house into a 10-key guesthouse. The success of the first Aleenta retreat has led to others in Phang Nga and Chiang Mai.

What were those early days like?
It was the beginning of the internet so I was just selling straight to the user at a price that nobody here could believe. We were full up half a year in advance because we were answering the gap in the market. Guests wanted to experience Thailand in comfort without having to stay in a large box or carry a backpack.

How do you pick your locations?
I don't like crowded places so we're never in the middle of the busy area. We're just a little bit outside. When I was looking to open another location after Pranburi, I looked everywhere for land that has a beachfront and I found it in Phang Nga. The one in Chiang Mai is at the foot of the mountain, next to a forest.

What do guests want from your businesses these days?
My first hotel in Pranburi has doubled in size to 20 rooms but we still don't have any televisions. I refuse to because we never had a TV when it was our beach house. When you're in a small property you can do that and we can tailor every experience for each guest.

Can a small luxury group compete with the big chains?
The playing field gets more and more levelled with each innovation. I said this 20 years ago and I can't believe that I'm still saying it. I can make a living against the big guys because my distribution is all system related and I can do more and more with technology.

GENERAL MANAGER
TED TUCKER
Aman Nai Lert Bangkok

Ted Tucker opened the first Aman in Bangkok in 2025, eight years after his first hospitality job in Thailand as part of the pre-opening team for the Ritz-Carlton, Koh Samui.

How did you start in hospitality?
I fell into it. In college I was studying theatre and I wanted to be on stage or writing scripts. I started working part time in the banqueting department at South Lodge, a luxury hotel in the south of England. There are some similarities between the two. Guests are your audience and you are putting on a show for them.

Hotel managers usually bounce around the world. Why have you decided to stay in Thailand?
My first impressions as a tourist made me want to work here and then the more I stayed, the more I knew I didn't want to leave. I fell more and more in love with it, rediscovering all of those things that made me curious in the first place and getting more of a profound understanding of Thai culture and the Buddhist way of life.

Has working in Thailand for nearly a decade changed you?
I am definitely a better person now than when I arrived. Living here teaches you to approach every day with a smile and to be calm and positive even in challenging situations.

What's the secret to Thai hospitality?
Service from the heart. Thais are caring by nature and they really want to make people feel welcome. It doesn't matter if you walk into a luxury hotel or a hole-in-the-wall restaurant. You are always greeted with a smile and a "wai" and you know that person will do their utmost to make sure you leave with a smile on your face too.

Thai cuisine is relished all over the world for its perfectly balanced flavours and fresh, aromatic ingredients. From distinguished dining to snappy street food, here is our list of the best culinary destinations in the land.

DRINKING & DINING

Spicy, sour, sweet, salty and bitter: Thai cuisine celebrates harmony and transforms meals into experiences that engage the senses. A trip to Thailand gives visitors an unmissable opportunity to try its food in all its wonderful regional varieties: when in the north try authentic *khao soi* (noodle soup); the centre of the country is famed for its sticky jasmine rice and refined royal cuisine; while in the south don't miss the abundance of seafood and bold, fiery curries. And you needn't fear going hungry at any hour: Thailand is renowned for its vibrant street food scene – from papaya salad to skewers of grilled chicken and beautifully prepared tropical fruit. The country also offers myriad drink options. A new generation of winemakers, brewers and distillers are making superb beverages and the cocktail scene is exceptional. Whether you have a taste for a never-to-be-forgotten fine-dining experience, a zingy salad or a delicious lemongrass-infused cocktail, we've got you covered. *Taan hai a-roi!*

THE EDIT

1 Restaurants
From sophisticated urban dining spots to sun-soaked beachfront restaurants.

2 Cafés, coffee shops & tea houses
Thailand takes its tea and coffee seriously – here's our pick of the best places to get your fix.

3 Street food
Everything from steaming bowls of *guay jub* to tossed noodles flamed up in woks.

4 Bars & jazz clubs
From jazz lounges in Bangkok to laid-back bars on the beach.

5 Sweet treats
Bean-to-bar chocolatiers, "stir-fried" ice cream and *khao niao mamuang* (mango sticky rice) – get your sweet tooth on.

6 Distilleries & wineries
Raise a glass to our pick of the best craft-spirit distilleries and innovative winemakers.

7 The experts
Three culinary insiders share their thoughts on the country's outstanding dining culture.

For bookings, see pages 216—218.

RESTAURANT
BO.LAN
Bangkok

Chefs Duangporn "Bo" Songvisava and Dylan Jones trained at Nahm, David Thompson's high-profile Thai restaurant in London. They showcase the breadth and complexity of Thailand's traditional recipes, rebuffing the notion of diluting flavours for softer palates. "We are committed to serving Thai food without compromise," says Jones. The ever-rotating menu harmonises with the seasons and lists dishes such as a red curry of grilled *Chachoengsao* duck with lychee, and sugarcane-steamed chicken. Bo.lan also shows how restaurants can serve the community: organic produce is sourced from small-scale farmers and you can pick up pantry staples from the on-site grocery.

RESTAURANT
CHARMKRUNG
Bangkok

This self-styled Thai tapas bar is a 60-cover establishment on the sixth floor of an unassuming building on Charoen Krung Road and is the sister restaurant of Charmgang and Charmkok, both of which are nearby. "Our menu is an eclectic mix of takes on Thai drinking snacks, old-school recipes that don't often make it onto menus and dishes that we have fun with, such as the Thai porchetta and *pani puri* with a crab salad," says Kiki Sontiyart, cofounder of Charmkrung. The restaurant takes its cues from Thai *kap klaem* ("drinking food") and Bangkok's multicultural identity, serving dishes that roam widely in influence but taste unmistakably Thai. Closing at 23.00, it's also the perfect spot for late-night dining.

RESTAURANT
GAGGAN
Bangkok

Few chefs embody reinvention like Gaggan Anand. The former drummer from Kolkata first shook up Bangkok's dining scene in 2010 with the original Gaggan, a restaurant widely hailed as one of the world's greatest. It closed in 2019 and he returned with a new culinary venture, which now operates under the same name. The centrepiece is a 14-seat chef's counter where a 25-course tasting menu unfolds below a disco ball, colourful lights and a thumping playlist. His cooking is rooted in progressive Indian cuisine but is layered with Thai and Japanese influences, a reflection of his life story. "I lived in India for 29 years, Thailand for 18 years and Japan changed the way I see food," he says.

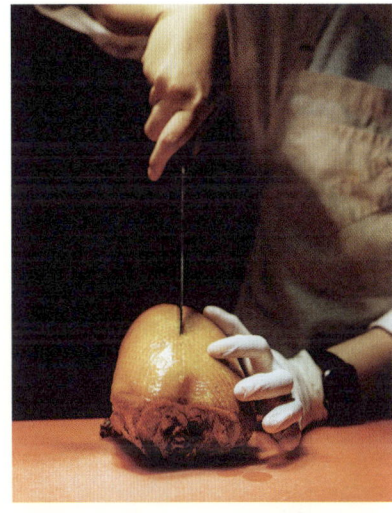

RESTAURANT
POTONG
Bangkok

A star of the country's culinary scene, this Thai-Chinese fine-dining restaurant holds a special place in the family history of chef and owner Pichaya "Pam" Soontornyanakij. She recommends the dry-aged duck – one of Potong's signature dishes – and the pad thai for a taste of innovation fused with tradition. Also worth trying is Potong's *sato*, a Thai rice wine brewed in-house. With her classical French training at the Culinary Institute of America and years spent working at acclaimed New York restaurant Jean-Georges, Soontornyanakij's fresh take on heritage Thai-Chinese cuisine isn't to be missed.

Just what the doctor ordered
Originally used as an apothecary that was first founded by Soontornyanakij's great-great-grandfather, the building where Potong is housed retains its restorative charm with a rooftop garden where guests can enjoy the sunset.

RESTAURANT
THIPSAMAI
Bangkok

It is claimed that this restaurant pioneered pad thai in 1939, when it was originally based on a canalboat. Now sited among the nightlife of Bangkok's Banglamphu district, Thipsamai offers a menu including mixed spring rolls and refreshing drinks such as Thai tea and juices squeezed on demand. We recommend the dish that started it all: the Superb Pad Thai. The noodles are cooked in shrimp oil, served with fresh deep-sea prawns and sheathed in a layer of egg that separates at the touch of a chopstick, releasing a plume of fragrant steam. Lime, beansprouts, peanuts and chilli flakes add to the taste. This, they claim, is how real pad thai should be made.

RESTAURANT
APPIA
Bangkok

When in Bangkok, there's plenty to try in terms of culinary enjoyment. Appia offers a journey to Rome's Testaccio neighbourhood without the airfare. Co-founded by chef Paolo Vitaletti (*pictured*) and restaurateur Jarrett Wrisley, this trattoria is Bangkok's top address for soulful Italian cuisine. Vitaletti grew up in a Roman butcher's family and brings that lineage to a menu that includes slow-cooked oxtail stew, tripe simmered in tomato, and the restaurant's signature porchetta rolled with liver, fennel pollen and rosemary. Pasta is made fresh daily, using methods taught by Vitaletti's mother and is served in a warmly lit interior lined with wine bottles. An open kitchen adds to the convivial mood.

RESTAURANT
BAAN DUSIT THANI
Bangkok

When the original Dusit Thani flagship was bulldozed for redevelopment, Benjarong and Thien Duong – two restaurants popular for Thai and Vietnamese cuisine, respectively – moved to this heritage house in nearby Saladaeng. "My grandmother loved Vietnamese food and Benjarong is a modern take on classical Thai dishes from all over the country," says Siradej Donavanik, vice-president of development at Dusit International and a third-generation family member. Originally, the idea was to move the two restaurants into a new hotel but Baan Dusit Thani's success has seen its current home become a permanent fixture. "We use this place to test out our ideas," says Donavanik.

RESTAURANT
BAAN TROK TUA NGORK
Bangkok

Having inherited a time-worn family property, the Assakul siblings – Win, Sun, Sandy and Sea – took five years to restore the 100-year-old building before bringing in a class of boundary-pushing restaurants and bars. Delia (see page 200) whips up Mexican fare, and Messengerservice crafts offbeat cocktails inspired by grocery staples. There's also The Living Room, a café-shop that offers respite from the beating tropical sun. It's worth seeking out Baan Trok Tua Ngork's creative residency programmes and events too. "By creating an entry point to Chinatown for many people, we've also helped to spotlight street food vendors, traditional shops and temples in the area," says Sun.

RESTAURANT
CURVY DINING
Bangkok

The light, bright, white flower-shaped pavilion that is Curvy Dining makes no apologies for its ultra-graphic presence in Bangkok's eastern reaches. Visitors are led towards the pavilion across a sequence of circular concrete platforms seemingly floating on a neat sea of green turf. Inside, tea, coffee and fruit-based drinks are on offer, alongside a menu of popular western dishes such as *spaghetti aglio olio e peperoncino*, Italian sausage with a rocket salad, nachos and chicken quesadillas. If you want a little pick-me-up, the affogato or the vanilla gelato will provide a welcome jolt of energy.

Flower power
The architects of the Curvy Dining building, Unknown Surface Studio, employed a radial organic geometry to create a structure with an exterior reminiscent of multiple petals. The interior is almost chapel-like, with curved white ribs rising to culminate in a skylight.

RESTAURANT
THE ARTISANS
Ayutthaya

The Artisans is a short drive from Ayutthaya's old town or a worthwhile day trip from Bangkok for fans of authentic cuisine served with a side of outstanding Thai architecture. Staple "village" dishes on the menu include clay-pot jasmine rice and charcoal-grilled salted fish. The riverside restaurant was designed by Bangkok-based architect Boonserm Premthada. Diners are spread spaciously across five triangular buildings made of wood-framed glass blocks. "I want our guests to feel like they are visiting a relative's home. Warm, relaxed and welcoming. Not overly polished, just real," says owner Sorawee Visitsopa.

Positive experience
The restaurant employs women from the local community to help preserve traditional cooking techniques and provides a steady income to these talented individuals. Owner Sorawee Visitsopa singles out the beef curry with cassia leaves: "This dish is a childhood memory. We used to eat it often but today it is hard to find."

RESTAURANT
RORSOR127
Nonthaburi

Rorsor127 is a unique dining experience found in the laid-back locale of Nonthaburi's Pak Kret district over the shoreline of the Chao Phraya river. Here, on a deck over the water, guests are served in a family or supper-club style, on a long, narrow table. A booking is required to secure a coveted spot but the intimacy of the venue means that patrons can converse with one another and enjoy their meal as wine is poured by the light of the setting sun. The restaurant's ethos that "every grain tells a story, every bite holds meaning and every meal is a quiet tribute to heritage and heart" is taken literally, with every dish having its own reason for being, relayed by the owner.

RESTAURANT
BAAN TA NID
Pathum Thani

Baan Ta Nid is a charming gem located a 45-minute drive north of Bangkok. As you head out, the city recedes and the landscape and housing appear to drift closer to the meandering Chao Phraya. In its riverside setting, the café offers indoor and outdoor seating. Guests dine on simple and flavoursome local cuisine and everything from fried shrimp and grilled catfish is on offer, all freshly caught. Though Bangkok has many riverside restaurants, few preserve an ambience that feels homely and true – and the menu attests to it. Punchy pork dishes and stir-fried vegetables accompany the kind of seafood dishes that are the perfect complement to the homely decor and the restful riverside location.

RESTAURANT
KAMSLA
Chiang Mai

Spinning plates
Chansukhon spends his evenings DJing at The House by Ginger (*see page 60*) and his days cooking multicourse lunches for fans of his contemporary take on northern Thai cuisine. If hanging out with such a talented individual sounds tempting, then Kamsla is a must.

Nassapong Chansukhon (*pictured*) – known to all as chef Nassa – set up his one-table restaurant in his garden in Saraphi. His lunch-only sittings must be booked in advance and cater for intimate parties of two to six people. The simple wooden dining table is surrounded by tropical plants and shielded by a canopy, while a brick structure houses the all-important grill. Kamsla serves tempting appetisers, followed by substantial platters that feature fresh prawns, fish and – the star of the menu – beef fat fried rice. This breath of fresh air on the Chiang Mai dining scene is a rare chance to eat delicious northern Thai food, cooked at home by a local.

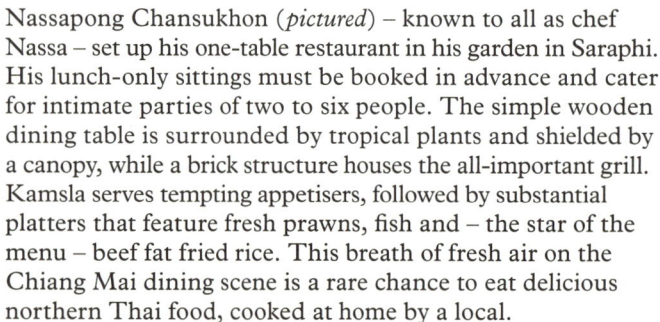

RESTAURANT
PRAÇA
Hua Hin

A playful interpretation of Thai street food in all its variety, this breezy hangout is part of The Standard, Hua Hin (*see page 23*), and resides in a heritage house, spilling onto a paved deck with front-row views of the beach. Diners can lounge at the ocean-facing wooden tables while conversing over Thai *izakaya*-style sharing plates – such as *krapao* tacos – and individual dishes, such as *tom yum goong* ramen (egg noodles, *onsen* eggs and black tiger prawns in a decadent sweet-and-sour soup). Come here early for the transition from afternoon tea to the evening, where inventive libations – try the tongue-in-cheek No More Mr Rice Guy – pair well with the sunset.

RESTAURANT
BLACKITCH ARTISAN KITCHEN
Chiang Mai

Chiang Mai has one of the most exciting culinary scenes in the country. Its street food and professional kitchens blend modern creativity with many ethnic heritages, including Lan Na and hill-tribe traditions. Phanuphol Bulsuwan (*pictured*), known as chef Black, opened his 18-seat restaurant on the second floor of a narrow city-centre shophouse, serving a 10-course menu adapted every three months according to the season. "Food is storytelling," says Bulsuwan. "Our jungle curry *kaeng paa* uses jackfruit in three forms wrapped in a taco shell in a reinterpretation of a central-style dish. The recipe uses traditional flavours and produce sourced nearby, interpreted through global techniques."

RESTAURANT
THE HOUSE BY GINGER
Chiang Mai

What better way to bring a day in Chiang Mai to a close than settling among the lush decor of The House by Ginger? The restaurant, lounge bar and two private dining rooms are expertly adorned with floral wallpaper, rattan chairs, velour Chesterfield lounges, Turkish rugs and low lighting. The atmosphere is the brainchild of Hans Bøgetoft Christensen, a Danish designer who moved to Chiang Mai in the late 1990s and set up design company The House in 2004, drawing on his professional background in fashion and homeware retailing. The menus feature accessible Thai favourites and if you're in need of a digestif, a similarly agreeable vibe awaits at The House Lounge, housed in a charming 1930s building.

RESTAURANT
ANOTHER SMITH
Tak

Bamboo is used to spectacular effect in this restaurant in northern Thailand. Around 40 varieties of the plant grow throughout the country and its strength and versatility make it a smart choice for everything from substantial structures to delicate finishes. At Another Smith, hefty columns, beams and rafters are crafted from bundles of large-diameter bamboo, while smaller blue-dyed sections have been used to line the ceiling. Arranged around a courtyard, the roofs of the two main wings lift in dynamic curves to create soaring ceilings for the dining spaces below. It all makes for a remarkable setting in which to enjoy the Thai-Chinese cuisine on offer. In between moments of admiring your surroundings, try the soft-shell crab fried with garlic, steamed river prawns with glass noodles, and the whole sea bass with black pepper.

RESTAURANT
LOCUS NATIVE
FOOD LAB
Chiang Rai

Kongwuth Chaiwongkachon (*pictured*) – known as chef
Kong – spent his early career gaining experience in French,
Japanese and Thai cuisine but it wasn't until he relocated to
Chiang Rai that he understood that culinary traditions in
the north feature ingredients and spice combinations that
set them apart from the south. Chef Kong celebrates these
contrasts at his 12-seat chef's table restaurant in a verdant
corner of Tatvani (*see page 26*). The set menu comes in two
parts: the first features creative interpretations of northern
Thai cuisine; the second – *khan tok* – is a traditional style of
serving multiple small plates on low-sided wooden trays.

Locus pocus
Even those jaded by fine dining are
bound to find a renewed appetite at
Locus Native Food Lab. The menu
comes complete with a QR code that
links to photographs of every dish
served, so cameras can stay in bags
and pockets.

RESTAURANT
KAEN
Khon Kaen

RESTAURANT
MA LONG DER
Chiang Rai

Nutrition and wellness expert Kanlayaphas Sittimuangai is the personification of her restaurant's central concept: food, art, health and eco-friendliness. This riverside spot doesn't stray far from authentic Lan Na fare and the care and creativity that goes into presentation means that dishes are as wonderful to look at as they are to eat. The menu offers plenty to keep the health-conscious happy, including the sticky rice, which consists of a multi-coloured mix of local varieties – yellow, red, white and blue – all wrapped in a banana leaf parcel. Grab a table on the terrace by the water, admire the sculptural ceiling featuring traditional weavings and fishing traps and enjoy a meal that lends a sense of indulgence to clean eating.

After a decade of working in the food industry together, Paisarn Cheewinsiriwat and Kanyarat "Jib" Thanomsaeng saw the opportunity to create their own place, putting emphasis on sourcing ingredients from suppliers as close to the restaurant as possible. "The local market dictates what we cook," says Jib. Their dish selection explores an array of Thai classics such as legs of beef cooked with chestnuts and jackfruit seeds in a vibrant *massaman* sauce, and sea bass baked in parchment with a herb broth. Careful consideration is also evident in the decor. "All the tables you see are from my dad's carpentry shop," says Cheewinsiriwat. "Each plate and set of cutlery is unique, crafted by local artisans."

MOK
Ubon Ratchathani

Named after the traditional Thai technique of steaming food, Mok is a converted two-storey home in Ubon Ratchathani. At its heart is chef Sirorat Thowtho – affectionately known as chef Fai or Auntie Chef (*pictured, above*). Ingredients are chosen with "the same care that a mother would take when cooking for her children", resulting in generous dishes that feel both nurturing and elevated. The herb-studded sea bass *mok* is a nod to the restaurant's name, while *mok pla ra* pairs fermented fish with pineapple relish and fresh vegetables. A Bib Gourmand nod affirms what locals already know: Mok is a heartfelt taste of Ubon Ratchathani's growing food scene.

RESTAURANT

KHAO KWAN
Koh Chang

Nongrut Noppawan's Khao Kwan has carved out a delicate niche for itself that contrasts with the more traditionalist culinary direction taken by many of Koh Chang's other restaurants. Serving small and colourful plates – often decorated with delicate bouquets of small flowers – the dishes erupt with flavour, from fragrant crab curry to garlic pepper scallops. A highlight from the many seafood options is the blue-spotted grouper, a local fish. "We try to elevate local ingredients and local recipes – while appealing to the crowd looking for a dose of Thai expertise in wellness," says Noppawan.

A sticky situation
Beyond the excellent seafood, guests come to Khao Kwan for the mango sticky rice, which, in keeping with the restaurant's polished presentation, is served in a coconut shell with coconut ice cream. All this inside a cosy spot that can accommodate no more than 50 diners.

RESTAURANTS

DISCOVER THAILAND

TREE TOPS SIGNATURE DINING
Koh Samui

Perched in a 120-year-old tree, this gourmet restaurant offers a unique perspective of Koh Samui. Nestled in the lush canopy, the venue's intricate network of skyline platforms supports eight private *salas*. The two-person tables are laid sparingly for the eight-course set menu. Indulge in oyster gratin with Thai caviar and charcoal-grilled wagyu coated in a Phraya rum-infused beef jus before finishing with the zesty lime-leaf sorbet. After dinner, stop off at the Singing Bird Lounge for a cocktail that celebrates nature's backing track. Named after the local wildlife, the drinks are designed to be enjoyed while taking in the surrounding birdsong. As the only treetop restaurant on the island, Tree Tops Signature Dining is perfect for a romantic dinner.

RESTAURANT

MARIA SEAVIEW RESTAURANT
Koh Panyee

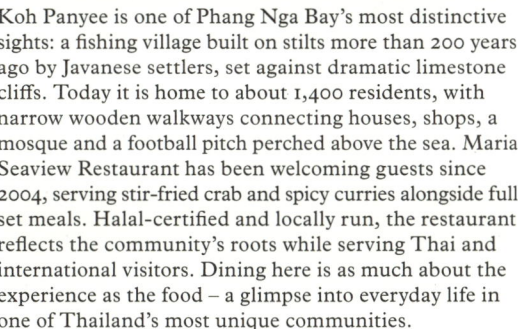

Koh Panyee is one of Phang Nga Bay's most distinctive sights: a fishing village built on stilts more than 200 years ago by Javanese settlers, set against dramatic limestone cliffs. Today it is home to about 1,400 residents, with narrow wooden walkways connecting houses, shops, a mosque and a football pitch perched above the sea. Maria Seaview Restaurant has been welcoming guests since 2004, serving stir-fried crab and spicy curries alongside full set meals. Halal-certified and locally run, the restaurant reflects the community's roots while serving Thai and international visitors. Dining here is as much about the experience as the food – a glimpse into everyday life in one of Thailand's most unique communities.

RESTAURANT
BLUE ELEPHANT
Phuket

The Blue Elephant is chef Nooror Somany Steppe's way of sharing Thai gastronomy with an international crowd. Set in the Phra Pitak Chinpracha mansion, this striking example of Sino-Portuguese architecture is fitted out with wicker furniture, along with ornate teak fittings complemented by European-style arches and original chequered tile flooring. But the food takes centre stage. "My mission is to preserve the essence of traditional Thai cuisine while adapting to modern culinary trends," says Somany Steppe. The main attraction is the Peranakan menu, an amalgamation of Hokkien-Chinese and Thai culinary traditions inspired by Phuketian heritage. Enjoy deep-sea tiger prawns served in a coconut shell or organic steamed crab dumplings – a traditional street food favourite.

RESTAURANT
SAMUT
Phuket

With a name that means "ocean" in Thai, Samut puts the riches of the sea at the heart of a multicourse tasting menu. Akkhapat Korsakul (*pictured*), known as chef Beer – of Bangkok's award-winning Le Du restaurant – and pastry chef Thitirat Kardkla, known as chef Ice, take guests on a gastronomic journey. Fresh catches are enhanced by local spices and prepared to southern taste. Banana shrimp and lobster can be found alongside tiger prawns and razor clams, all of which are best polished off with traditional Phuket dessert *tu bo*, which features root vegetables and coconut cream. The intimate Chinese-style dining room has just five tables but the offerings are expansive: the river prawn and shiitake mushroom rice is a standout.

TU KAB KHAO
Phuket

Even though Tu Kab Khao's name refers to a small pantry used for storing leftovers, the irony is that most plates here head back to the kitchen clean and clear. The menu is an ode to traditional southern Thai cuisine, combining a heady mix of aromatic spices, succulent meats and vibrant colours. The *gaeng som pla* (a local fish coated in turmeric sauce) has a signature spicy-sour flavour, and for those looking to ease into the Thai palate, the *sen mee gaeng poo* (crab curry) is a milder alternative. Draped curtains, arched doorways and velvet sofas set a plush tone inside this heritage house but the most striking feature has to be the giant blue crustacean installation that clings to the building's exterior. Wonderfully kitsch, it's a great conversation starter and has become a homing device for diners seeking excellent regional fare.

CAFÉ
YELLOW LANE
Bangkok

Champion of breakfasts
Founder (and fan of smashed avocado) Marc C Close is originally from Brisbane but moved to Bangkok more than a decade ago to build a tech company that he later sold. "It gave me the resources to do what I'm doing now," says Close, who continues to run his business from an office at Yellow Lane. Close eats there regularly: "I'm probably the number-one customer," he says.

An Aussie-flavoured, all-day restaurant housed in one of Ari's typical mid-century modernist houses, Yellow Lane is a popular gathering spot in this leafy residential neighbourhood in north Bangkok. Staple brunch dishes on the ever-evolving menu lean heavily on eggs, avocado and "things on toast". Food is served alongside an extensive programme of activities, including live music, art exhibitions, film screenings and yoga workshops. There's even a popular *onsen* and ice bath out back, where a mix of expats and Thais come to mingle and make full use of the lush grounds of this inviting two-storey former family home.

CAFÉ
HARUDOT
Chon Buri

Overseen by Thai practice IDIN Architects (an acronym for Integrating Design into Nature), this café for Nana Coffee Roasters houses large trees, including a 100-year-old baobab, distinctive for its bottle-shaped trunk. Harudot attracts visitors with its razor-sharp look featuring black timber cladding and pointed roofs, and keeps them seated with its extensive offerings. Inside, take your pick from the "speed bar", complete with an espresso machine, or the "slow bar", where baristas hand-pour speciality brews. Once you've had your caffeine fix, be sure to browse the varied menu of savoury dishes and sweet treats. With generous opening hours, guests can enjoy indoor and outdoor seating from sunrise until sunset.

CAFÉ
KHAGEE
Chiang Mai

It's easy to inadvertently walk straight past Khagee as you navigate the busy traffic. But Khagee, owned and run by Thai-Japanese couple Thames and Miki, is the perfect antidote to the swarms of scooters and gaggles of children from the secondary school next door. With white-painted brick walls, gauzy linen curtains and an assortment of contemporary and vintage furniture, Khagee feels breezy and bright. Everything is freshly handmade using Miki's recipes, with both Asian and European-style treats baked each day, all neatly arranged and temptingly displayed at the entrance. We recommend the mini cylinders of carrot cake topped with cream cheese icing.

CAFÉ
CAP
Chanthaburi

Cap stands for "Café and People", a name inspired by the drive to provide the area with a wholesome, modern hang-out spot. Greenery lines its welcoming entrance and the property stretches past the busy barista's box towards a small, well-lit courtyard that offers seating for patrons. Cap's owner, the older half of a pair of entrepreneurial siblings, runs her business on the opposite side of the street to her younger brother's project. His spot, known as Easterly (*see page 75*), is the antithesis to Cap's strictly by-day activities, leaning as it does towards dining and nightlife. Cap, a staple of Chanthaburi old town, draws a consistent crowd of coffee-drinking disciples, with some even sporting the café's merchandise.

CAFÉ
THE GARDENER
Chanthaburi

Husband-and-wife founders of The Gardener, Chaiwat and Pinyapat Treeratsakulchai – the former an architect – left the intensity of the Thai capital to move to Pinyapat's hometown. "I couldn't live in Bangkok anymore; it's too busy," says Chaiwat. Here, they designed a comfortable, elegant café tucked among a string of shops near the Chanthaburi river, featuring walls hung with framed prints and an interior full of lush plants, where customers can drop in for a leisurely pick-me-up, many taking the time to enjoy the serene environment to sketch, read a book and relax. As well as hot drinks, the café offers an array of sweet treats and frozen smoothies, emphasising the natural elements from which it earns its name.

CAFÉ
EASTERLY
Chanthaburi

Motion graphics designer Khanapong Pumarin established this local winner with the specific aim of channeling the community feel of a social club into a café that moonlights as a bar. The concept and the smart interior – a timeless mix of bare brick, wood and exquisite lighting – has proved a success among young locals. By day, you can grab a coffee; at night, espresso martinis go well with the entertainment, including DJs and guest mixologists. Even though it changes often, the wine list is of consistently high quality and the small plates are vibrant. There are even rooms for overnight stays. Cap (*see page 74*), a coffee shop run by Pumarin's older sister, sits across the road.

COFFEE SHOP
KARO
Bangkok

Karo has been the hottest spot for a casual hangout since its opening. Set in the residential Pridi neighbourhood, the space's stripped-back concrete walls and lofty ceilings give it an industrial edge, softened by the relaxed atmosphere and tables that spill out under shaded awnings. On any given day, a stream of locals (including Bangkok's governor) and tourists stop in for a well-poured coffee or something sweet. Sri Lankan-born founder Karo Iyash taught himself to roast, favouring speciality blends from single-origin beans and keeping coffee "simple, so it can be enjoyed by all". The menu rewards curiosity, with standouts such as the homemade Ceylon cinnamon rolls, topped with buttery frosting.

COFFEE SHOP
ROOTS
Bangkok

Roots is one of Thailand's most respected speciality roasters and now has 12 cafés around the capital. The brand was founded with a mission to build links between coffee drinkers and the people who grow, process and roast the beans. The approach is simple: great coffee brewed with beans carefully chosen to best fit your taste. Roots takes pride in its farm-to-cup approach, in which it showcases Thai producers, with beans changing regularly to highlight different regions and flavours. Every type of coffee has a card detailing its origin, tasting notes and producer information. Pet-friendly and always buzzing, this is a perfect spot to connect and caffeinate in good company.

TEA HOUSE
CITIZEN TEA CANTEEN
Bangkok

Once you step across the threshold of Citizen Tea Canteen – decorated in a brilliant interplay of orange, white and black tiles – your senses will be overwhelmed. There are artworks, bright textiles, silk screens, local crafts and examples of striking original furniture, such as handmade chairs with colourful woven cushions. All of this vibrancy is packed within a traditional wooden shophouse in Talat Noi, near Chinatown. There's also a counter in the corner that is reminiscent of an old-school tea shop and offers a wide variety of tea blends sourced from farms across Thailand. The hot duck soup tea is a particular highlight.

Time for tea
Citizen Tea Canteen splits the difference between a traditional Chinese tea house and a colourful, eclectic showroom. "We're paying homage to Chinatown and its roots," says veteran craftsman and designer Saran Yen Panya, who brought the space to life. "I wanted to create a showroom where people can soak up new experiences."

TEA HOUSE
SANGKAEW
Chiang Rai

The rolling hills outside Chiang Rai city that host tea
shop Sangkaew are a place to step outside of time. "We
convey stories through the design of our tea house and
guest rooms," says owner Puriwat Wicha. In the balmy
afternoons you can enjoy Burmese tea – picked on the
family plantation in Myanmar's Kengtung region – and
a tray of Kengtung and northern Thai specialities, while
dipping your toes in the adjacent stream. For the full
experience, make a pre-booking for dinner to catch the
sun setting behind the hills and feast on spicy northern-
style curries, noodle bowls and sizzling grill dishes. And if
you fall in love with the place, book into one of their Lan
Na-style wooden guest rooms for the night.

TEA HOUSE

SAWANBONDIN TEA HOUSE & EXPERIENCE
Chiang Rai

On a gravel lane in the outskirts of Chiang Rai city, Sawanbondin – which translates as "heaven on Earth" – is a stylish tea house that encourages quiet appreciation of its brews, from roasted green tea and Oriental Beauty oolong to its own award-winning Single Origin Mae Ai First Flush black tea. "Our aspiration is to make this world a 'heaven on Earth' for everyone," says founder Chukiat Vasaruchapong (*pictured*). Heavenly desserts made from local ingredients such as riceberry are also available, alongside scoops of matcha gelato that are perfect for combating the sizzling hot-season temperatures.

Oolong and prosper
The mountains between the city and Myanmar's border are ideal for tea cultivation and Sawanbondin sources leaves from local community forests where biodiversity is carefully preserved. "Sawanbondin is envisioned as a bridge between people and the environment," says Vasaruchapong.

IN FOCUS
STREET FOOD
Get it while it's hot

1 2

3

Wok this way
Street food in Thailand comes in an
endless variety of forms – including but
by no means limited to grilled or tossed
noodles and ingredients flamed up in
woks. A lot of these are techniques and
recipes passed through generations,
akin to family secrets.

4

1 Fresh herbs make all the difference
2 Takeaway with a smile
3 Unusual textures
4 24-hour dining
5 Hot wheels
6 Made while you watch
7 Just one or two more

5   6

Unapologetically bold and flavourful, Thailand's kerbside dining culture is a deeply rooted part of its heritage. With busy chefs at the helm, tables scattered on the pavement and locals bookending their days at local street-food vendors, there is something timeless and even exciting about being right in the middle of the bustle.

Food has a way of bridging divides and Thai street food has done this for generations. From tucked-away noodle stalls selling family favourites to *khao gaeng* shops that provide a place of refuge during lunch hours, street food in Bangkok and beyond offers convenience and the comforts of home cooking in an increasingly urbanised environment.

Bangkok is incredibly proud of its rightly famous street-food tradition. There are endless options – from places only neighbourhood locals know to some that are featured in the Michelin Guide – whether you're involved in some late-night exploring in Chinatown looking for steaming bowls of *guay jub* or walking through bustling Sukhumvit on the hunt for pork noodle soup.

No matter how quickly things move here, the street-food vendors will always be a constant, with the same unpretentious service: water served in aluminium mugs and hot plates of delicious food.

7

BAR
FREAKING OUT THE NEIGHBOURHOOD
Bangkok

Inspired by visits to Tokyo's audiophile listening bars, Bangkok couple James and Kiratra Gilbody, with Jitti Promosaka Na Sakolnakorn, opened their own indie-leaning venue for serious music appreciation. Freaking Out the Neighbourhood, which is outfitted with high-end audio geekery in the form of vintage JBL speakers and a McIntosh amp, treats each night like a festival line-up, playing a mix of acts ahead of the night's featured album. "We play it start to finish, how the artist intended it to be heard," says James. The intimate 22-seat space has a music-inspired cocktail menu for patrons digging the mix of indie, psych-rock and the occasional punk release, plus a retail space for records and hip music merch.

BAR
THE NORM
Bangkok

The Norm's outdoor terrace looks out over downtown Bangkok but there are plenty of distractions to be found inside. The wood-panelled interior was designed by Thai architecture studio Ekar and Fritz Hansen provided the furniture. On big nights, the decks will be spinning in two venues at once: The Main Hall and The Terrace, The Norm's outdoor spritz bar. The Whispering Room – a speakeasy that serves Japanese whisky and plays vinyl jazz – provides a more intimate atmosphere. Everything about The Norm, from the music to the dress code has been designed to make the rooftop bar feel inviting. "We are in a super-expensive building but I don't want this to feel too exclusive," says founder Sitthan "Turk" Sa-Nguankun.

BAR
TEP BAR
Bangkok

Entering this restored shophouse in the Soi Nana quarter of Bangkok's Chinatown is to be immersed in a compelling fusion of traditional cuisine and modern hospitality. A dimly lit courtyard leads to the main space, where live performances on traditional Thai instruments fill the air with an inviting beat. The stripped-back interior, all bare concrete and minimal furnishings, subtly highlights the building's old bones, while the cocktail list reinterprets local classics such as *ya dong*, a traditional Thai herbal spirit. Foodwise, guests can enjoy small plates of freshly grilled meat and fish dishes inspired by Bangkok street food, as well as plant-based options. It's no wonder that this spot nicknamed itself the "cultural bar of Thailand".

BAR
RUSTY-SOCIAL CLUB
Khon Kaen

At the heart of Khon Kaen's thronged central district, Rusty-Social Club makes a solid case for being the most-frequented bar-club in the city. During the week, it takes on a tempered and classic live-music vibe. At weekends, you'll probably need to join the queue to secure a coveted spot inside. Open from 18.00 to 01.00, the venue attracts crowds bolstered by the large student population come to hear the most thrilling new local acts performing original music and covers of smash-hit singalongs on the sizeable stage. With two well-stocked bars, you won't need to disappear for long before diving back into the action. There's a garden at the back where young crowds catch their breath before heading into the night.

BAR

HOUSE OF SUZY
Koh Samui

British-born New Zealander William Norbert-Munns relocated to Koh Samui in 2021, as the strain of running more than 20 business ventures in Cambodia encouraged him to seek out a slower pace of life. "We came in search of fresh air, space and the kind of island rhythm where a family can thrive," he says. Unable to sit idle for long, the entrepreneur opened House of Suzy, a cocktail bar that caters for the creative residents of Lamai. It features deep burgundy tones and soft lighting in a sultry interior that is a nod to mid-century Shanghai, with a menu including handmade dim sum alongside reinvented classic cocktails. Expansion may be on the horizon, but for now, the island bar and its charismatic owner are bringing warmth, charm and style to their small corner of the island.

BAR
COCO TAM'S
Koh Samui

Coco Tam's is among a growing number of restaurants tempting Koh Samui's visitors to venture out of their five-star villas. The rustic setting attracts a relaxed crowd with its palm-thatched roof and front-row seats to the island's enchanting sunsets. "Every corner has been lovingly crafted to draw you in," says owner Chawanan "Tam" Chotechurangkool. Ambient music sets the tone as guests indulge in juicy burgers, wood-fired pizzas and grilled seafood platters. Come evening, guests spill onto the beachfront with drinks in hand for the renowned fire show. A spectacle of sparks and flames, the performance leans into the island's reputation as a party hot spot.

JAZZ CLUB
ALONE TOGETHER
Bangkok

JAZZ CLUB
SMALLS
Bangkok

A sultry, eccentric space, Smalls is a go-to spot for an evening of jazz in the heart of Bangkok's Sathorn district. It hosts a rich mix of Thai musicians and international talent. For a night spent alfresco, head to the second floor, where a balcony offers views over the surrounding neighbourhood. "Smalls has a layered atmosphere," says co-owner Bruno Tanquerel. "Part-art bar, part-jazz club, part-nighttime refuge, it has a loyal crowd and unpredictable charm." The menu is just as eclectic, featuring house-made rillettes and saucisson, fish and chips, quesadillas and Thai fare. "We aim to keep an intimate space that encourages slow conversation and connection," says Tanquerel.

Low seating and attentive table service at Alone Together, an intimate jazz bar in Sukhumvit, encourage guests to enjoy the immersive experience with a cocktail in hand. "There's no elevated stage," says founder Sitthan "Turk" Sa-Nguankun, a trained-musician-turned Bangkok bar impresario. "Our musicians perform on the same level as the audience, bringing a shared presence to the room." To keep things feeling fresh, the music schedule is deliberately kept flexible and decided on a weekly basis. Jazz musicians regularly play with those from other genres. "We work closely with local musicians to create line-ups that feel organic and alive," says Turk, who also occasionally plays when the moment feels right.

CHOCOLATE SHOP
KAD KOKOA
Bangkok

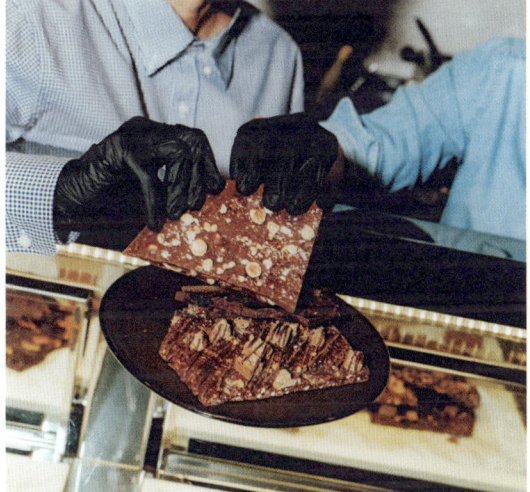

CHOCOLATE SHOP
KANVELA
Chiang Mai

It's a common Chiang Mai story: a local boy goes to Bangkok to make a career and ends up returning to his hometown to reconnect with his roots. Once back, and looking to start a new business, Kanvela founder Thana Kunaraksvong found that cacao trees flourished in the northern climate and the amount of quality time he got to spend with his family increased. This led to an award-winning tree-to-bar chocolate business founded on ethical and fair-trade farming practices. "Our philosophy states that Kanvela is where quality meets community," Thana says. From solid bars such as *awl-doi* citrus milk chocolate to intricately decorated bonbons, the range leans on Thai spices and herbs to create a range of distinct flavours.

Kad Kokoa's journey to becoming the gold standard of Thai chocolate began with a shop in Sathorn staffed by husband and wife Paniti and Nuttaya Junhasavasdikul. The pair are both lawyers in Bangkok but became interested in chocolate after acquiring a plot of farmland in northern Thailand and ended up becoming pioneers of the country's burgeoning single-origin chocolate trade. Kad Kokoa's flagship café in Bangkok opened in 2018 and the two-storey building in a quiet part of Sathorn is made out of several wooden rice barns that the Junhasavasdikuls transported from Chiang Mai. The on-site kitchen continues to make the chocolate bars, cookies, bonbons and ice cream served to the café's customers.

ICE CREAM SHOP
ROCKET ICE CREAM
Chanthaburi

Frozen in the past
Establishments with real dessert heritage in Thailand are few and far between but Rocket has more than 50 years of gelaterie experience. It also boasts a genuine place in local culinary history – it was the first parlour in Chanthaburi to adopt the use of machinery for the production of ice cream.

Rocket Ice Cream is a shiny spot in Chanthaburi, with fridges situated below an open window overlooking the street. Staff periodically emerge from within, waving a beckoning hand to encourage passers-by to grab a refreshing fix. Durian, milk and Thai iced tea are among the plethora of fun and innovative flavours on offer, forming a frozen mosaic of multicoloured ice creams. We recommend taking a seat in the parlour's quaint dining space to enjoy your tasty frozen treat and escape the midday heat before taking a leisurely stroll through the meandering backstreets of the Old Town.

ICE CREAM SHOP
TORRY'S
Phuket

Inside an attractive pastel-pink Sino-Portuguese shophouse in Phuket's Old Town, Torry's pulls in visitors with premium Phuketian flavours that can't be found elsewhere. The traditional Bi-Co-Moi dessert (a glutinous black rice) is reimagined in a dish with coconut ice cream. Other difficult-to-resist flavours include red bean, *bee pang* and yuzu. Phuket native Torry Wongwattanakit is to thank for such ingenuity. "It is a love story about one's roots, retelling heritage through ice cream," he says. Want to bring something home with you? The traditional mooncake biscuits, encased in whimsical blue-and-white packaging, make for excellent gifts.

DESSERT SHOP
BA HAO TIAN MI
Bangkok

The circular granite entrance is what you spot first, the golden glow from the counter at the back gently luring you into this neighbourhood secret. An offshoot of a hole-in-the-wall bar dreamed up by a group of friends, Ba Hao Tian Mi is a new-wave dessert parlour that reimagines Thai-Chinese sweet treats for a modern palate, welcoming locals and tourists alike over bowls of gojiberry pudding and black sesame soup with taro mochi. Six locations have opened since the first one in 2019, including the Central Chidlom department store and Central Ladprao shopping centre. "We have expanded beyond puddings and into a wide array of desserts, including milk tea and pastries," says cofounder Karnchanit Charoenyos.

DISTILLERY
THE DISTILLERY PHUKET
Phuket

Having experienced the 2004 tsunami, Marine Lucchini was deeply moved by the kindness of the Thai people. "From that moment, I knew I wanted to come back and build something meaningful," she says. Alongside a group of entrepreneurs, including Thibault Spithakis, Lucchini made use of her background in premium wine and spirits and soon made her mark by launching rum label Chalong Bay. At the company's distillery, visitors are shown behind the scenes on hourly tours before they are invited to dine at the bamboo-clad, farm-led bistro and then shake up their own cocktails.

WINERY & VINEYARD

GRANMONTE ESTATE
Khao Yai

Khao Yai is known for its national park but it has cultivated another draw: wine. At the heart of this shift is Granmonte Estate, where husband-and-wife team Visooth and Sakuna Lohitnavy opened a vineyard. The family moved here in 1999 with daughters Nikki and Mimi, experimenting with syrah and chenin blanc to suit the valley's winters. Today, Nikki – one of Asia's few female oenologists – produces bottles labelled 100 per cent Khao Yai-grown. "We wanted something to stand shoulder to shoulder with wines of the world," says Mimi. Visitors can stay for a lunch at Vincotto, where dishes such as lamb shank in red-wine jus reveal how far Khao Yai wine has come.

Estate of the nation
Granmonte Estate's original 1999 plot was a 16-hectare patch that had formerly been a cashew orchard. The label's first vintage was bottled in 2001 and the winery was expanded over the years with a further 14 hectares. The estate's wines were served to world leaders at the 2022 Asia-Pacific Economic Cooperation conference hosted in Thailand.

Thailand's culinary scene has a history that goes back a thousand years – and a future that celebrates regional ingredients and dishes using contemporary techniques. We hear from three seasoned professionals in the industry.

MEET THE EXPERTS

CHEF

VARESARA "BIC" SMITASIRI
Khua Kling Pak Sod

Varesara "Bic" Smitasiri left a corporate career to guide her family's Bangkok restaurant from small cookhouse to a successful brand known for serving spicy fare from her mother's hometown of Tha Sae in southern Thailand's Chumphon province.

How did your relationship with food start?
I was very lucky that, on weekends, my mum and auntie used to take me to local food markets instead of big department stores. My dad worked in hotels and he always wanted to select the best things for us, starting with the food that we ate together. It was his dream to open his own restaurant.

Can you recommend a market worth visiting?
I love Or Tor Kor in Bangkok. They source the best. We've been using the same suppliers for 20 years. It's expensive but it's a long-term relationship. For southern ingredients, my mum's family sends them to me.

What characterises southern Thai cuisine?
Intense spiciness that comes from a blend of peppers and chillis in the curry paste. Southern curries are darker and more intense than central Thai curries, often featuring seafood. The base is shrimp paste with fish sauce adding saltiness and we use a lot of turmeric, fingerroot, ginger and *bai liang* – the queen of southern vegetables.

MIXOLOGIST
POP DIREKRITTKUL
Eat Me

CHEF
WEERAWAT "NUM" TRIYASENAWAT
Samuay & Sons

Eat Me restaurant is something of a Bangkok institution, attracting customers for 28 years despite being hidden in a small downtown *soi* (side street). While the modern "borderless" cuisine is rightly lauded, it's the inspired Sip Some Thai cocktail menu of award-winning mixologist Pop Direkrittkul that dares to experiment with local flavours. We asked him for some Thai tipple tips.

Does Thai food lend itself well to making cocktails?
Some dishes, sure. I've tried to make cocktails from many dishes and it's taken around eight years to get to the final version of the cocktail menu. White spirits work best with Thai food.

Thai cuisine has some powerful flavours. How do you make sure you don't overpower the drink?
For our signature Laab Moo (spicy pork salad) cocktail, we infuse vodka with toasted rice then add local Thai herbs. We add just a few drops of strong flavours such as fish sauce or soy sauce, using them like bitters.

What do you enjoy the most about your job?
Every night is a challenge. Many people ask us to mix them a special cocktail so we use our experience to make them something unique.

Which cocktail would you try in a bar to see if they know what they're doing?
I'd start with their signature cocktail and see how the flavours work together. Then I'd try a dry martini. If that's good, then the bar is good.

Weerawat "Num" Triyasenawat and his brother opened Samuay & Sons in their hometown of Udon Thani in Isan, close to the border with Laos. They named the restaurant after their "hero" mother, a tailor who runs her dress shop nearby.

What's on the menu?
Healthy home-style cooking using seasonal and local produce as much as possible. We're focused on regional Isan cuisine.

Why is Isan cuisine growing in popularity around Thailand?
It's comfort food. It's more rustic than the other regions' cuisines and it's very simple to cook. *Pla ra* (fermented fish) is the main seasoning and then we have two favourite spices, *khao khua* (toasted rice powder) and *prik bon* (chilli flakes).

What's the idea behind "som tam" – papaya salad – the region's most famous dish?
Tam som is a particular word in Laos and Isan. *Tam* means to pound something and *som* means sour. That's the concept and it can be applied to any fruit that has a sour or tangy flavor, including papaya, mangoes and Cape gooseberries. Bruise them up and season with *pla ra*.

Tell us about Isan's seasonal produce.
The soil is very dry and doesn't hold much water when it rains, so we have learnt how to survive on fermented fish, edible plants, sticky rice and insects. People enjoy eating ant eggs in summer – they're considered a delicacy. During the rainy season, it's all about mushrooms and bamboo shoots; in winter, it's fish and the new rice after harvest.

The shopping-and-design scene in Thailand reflects centuries of cultural exchange, regional identities and everyday creativity, providing keen shoppers with plenty to peruse. These are the places where you should spend your baht.

DESIGN & RETAIL

Thailand has a formidable reputation as a regional leader for graphic, product and furniture design, as well as for fashion. Exploring this singular scene is not just an opportunity to take home something special but it also offers a window into the country's cultural soul and modern spirit. At one end of the spectrum, Bangkok is home to vast shopping centres that serve as air-conditioned public spaces selling goods ranging from luxury brands to fresh produce. Elsewhere in the city, making the effort to find your way to studios, workshops and independent boutiques pays dividends in the quality and variety available. Whether it's silk textiles, classic earthenware or the jewel-coloured pressed metal cups seen in every market, there is a glorious diversity to Thai craft and design. Beyond the capital, Chiang Mai is rich with high-quality traditional products and is also home to a new generation of designers and makers using local materials and time-honoured techniques. Leave room in your bag – you're going to need it.

THE EDIT

1   Fashion
Spots to refresh your wardrobe with haute couture, local streetwear and relaxed island apparel.

2   Concept stores
Five shops with an expert approach to curating (and making) their wares.

3   Specialists
From silk pillowcases to handcrafted ceramics: a list of artisans that are the best at what they do.

4   Malls & markets
Pick up clothing, homewear, wellness products and Thai trinkets at these bustling retail hubs.

5   The experts
We meet some Thai entrepreneurs and learn about their inspirations and experiences.

For details, see pages 216—218.

FASHION
THE DECORUM
Bangkok

Mixing things up

Following success at home, and driven by the notion of moving things to the next stage, The Decorum has opened in Singapore, launched a private label, expanded into womenswear with a separate shop in the Gaysorn Amarin shopping centre and introduced a concept store – Club Luminaries – championing brands such as Universal Overall and J Press.

At the centre of Bangkok's growing community of style-savvy locals sits The Decorum. Co-founders Sirapol "Guy" Ridhiprasart and Warong "Ball" Phattharachaikul started off by selling Japanese-made Kamakura shirts from a space originally designed to be Guy's home. Today, the retailer caters to all aspects of a modern wardrobe, with a stock that includes made-to-measure suiting hand-sewn by tailors in South Korea, shoes from UK labels Baudoin & Lange and Crockett & Jones, Echizenya trousers and socks by Bresciani. The considered mix has won over businessmen and high-fashion obsessives alike.

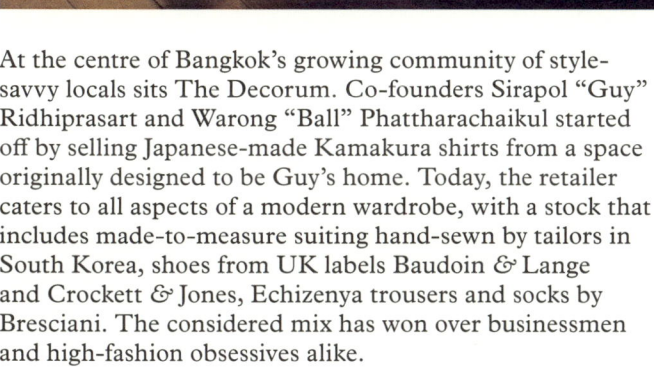

FASHION
JBB
Bangkok

Before Jirawat "Bote" Benchakarn (*pictured*) debuted his menswear label in 2007, clothes shopping in Bangkok tended to be limited to looking through drab, ill-fitting business attire sold in department stores. "There was a big gap in the market," says Bote, who started out designing the kind of well-cut shirts that he wanted to wear, before quickly expanding to signature blazers and pleated trousers. At his shop, you can slip into some comfortable linen tailoring and breathable Oxford button-downs cut to accentuate a strong silhouette. There are informal pieces too, such as safari jackets inspired by Yves Saint Laurent. Bote's own style is also a point of reference, namely the chinos he used to wear two or three sizes too big with a tight belt when he was a fashion student at San Francisco's Academy of Art University. About 80 per cent of JBB's fabrics come from Japan, with the remainder sourced in Italy and South Korea. "Menswear, for me, is very technical. There isn't a lot of detail, so it all comes down to the fit, fabric and finish."

FASHION
ASAVA
Bangkok

Once an Asava collection drops, shoppers arrive in droves to secure the latest designs by Polpat "Moo" Asavaprapha, one of Thailand's leading fashion figures. After studying at Parsons School of Design in New York and spending seven years as a fashion director at Max Mara, Moo returned home to Bangkok to launch this womenswear label – known for its sleek silhouettes crafted from delicate Thai silk – in 2008. Since then, he's also worked on his uniform-design department, with his creations for Bangkok Airways being of particular note. "The uniform is a walking form of advertising for the brand. The colours make it friendly and approachable," says Moo, who also has a restaurant, Sava Dining, in his business mix.

FASHION
VVON SUGUNNASIL
Bangkok

Bangkok's fashionable crowd heads to Vvon Sugunnasil for bespoke suits, formal gowns and other outfits for one-off occasions. Founder Thattaworn "Von" Sugunnasil (*pictured*) conducts regular fittings at his showroom and atelier in Sathorn while also creating fetching uniforms for some of the Thai capital's best hotels. The label was established in 2014 and introduced a popular ready-to-wear collection in 2019. The showroom is housed in a standalone two-storey house opposite the Austrian ambassador's official residence, converted from family home to fashion maison by Siriyot Chaiamnuay of Onion (*see page 192*). "This feels like my home," says Von, who keeps the space quiet and private for focused fittings.

FASHION
LONG GOY
Chiang Mai

FASHION
PALIT
Chiang Mai

Long Goy's studio, showroom and shop is, unusually for a fashion house, set in a residential neighbourhood near Chiang Mai, among rice fields, canals and small houses. The two-storey building with its bright blue façade – designed by Chiang Mai-based architects Sher Maker (*see page 193*) – makes a striking statement. Designer Supakorn Sunkanaporn (*pictured, left*) employs laser-cut stencils, then uses a subtraction process to remove dye from areas of each piece of clothing. The cut and fit of Sunkanaporn's garments, with their boxy, straight silhouettes, patch pockets and big dramatic pleats, provide the perfect base for his unique approach to contemporary fashion with a distinctive Thai twist.

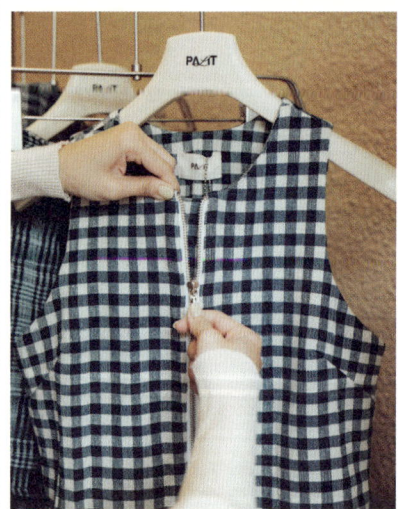

Clothing in black, grey, white, cream and indigo, and textiles made from hand-woven, hand-dyed cotton are seductively arranged in Palit's shop in Chiang Mai. Palit started out with beautiful macramé and crochet bags but it's the clothing made from natural fibres that epitomise the brand today. Lightweight cotton tops, dresses, skirts and trousers for women offer comfort in tropical conditions but simple elegance is never compromised. Clever details such as asymmetrical cuts and ruched silhouettes are the perfect accompaniment to the beauty and tactility of the hand-made fabrics. A range of accessories, alongside textiles for the home, are designed to complement the clothing and bring an extra touch of Palit panache.

FASHION
ES PHUKET
Phuket

ES Phuket is a melting pot of contemporary fashion trends and traditional Thai designs. Introducing bold patterns and vivid colours, the boutique stocks brands that revamp tired beach clothing, giving it a new lease of life that reflects Phuket's vibrant culture. In a building buried in the crowded streets of Talat Nuea, the main shop floor features metal railings that line cream walls, allowing the garments to take centre stage. In the room's centre, a dark wooden table showcases finely-wrought crocheted accessories and a quaint seating area awaits tired legs. "We are dedicated to exclusively selling Thai labels," says owner Wisa Thongtan. "I want to showcase the talent, creativity and quality that locals have to offer."

FASHION
PAINT PALETTE
Phuket

In an ornate Sino-Portuguese shophouse on Thalang Road, Wanrawee "Tudtu" Temtripeth (*pictured, below*) runs a "tropical concept store" that has made a name for crafting clothing and accessories that incorporate intricate patterns and rich colours, such as linen shirts with shell detailing, woven rattan bags and seagrass hats. Tudtu's mission to revitalise the area's handicraft traditions means that the label's creations are the work of local artisans. "Paint Palette has given us the opportunity to share products created by Thai craftspeople with travellers from all over the world," says Tudtu. The same spirit is found at nearby sister sites Tropical Sunshine and Canvas, which are also rich in handmade resortwear.

CONCEPT
WAREHOUSE 30
Bangkok

Found less than a 20-minute walk from Chinatown, Warehouse 30 is a tasteful enclave of retail and design units that unfold via a long corridor threading each consecutive plot together. The site is a former warehouse for machinery and locomotive parts, with the original concrete, exposed beams and steel structure still in place. The unified layout of Warehouse 30 means that you can neatly weave from a streetwear pop-up event in Carnival, a shoe shop and clothing retailer, into A Coffee Roaster by Li-bra-ry to grab a special-roast V60 to accompany your perusal of installations by Thai artists at 333Gallery or Gallery Curu. A bite to eat, crafts for the home and other shopping opportunities are also on offer.

CONCEPT
PANA OBJECTS
Bangkok

Pana Objects is mostly dedicated to one material: wood. Most of the product range consists of measured, well-executed examples of homewares. "It's a very special medium," says Pattarapong Pornpanapong, one of Pana Objects' founders. "Every piece of wood grain is unique – and having once been part of a tree, there's a warmth and simplicity to the material that brings a sense of calm." Since opening in 2010, the brand has evolved. While it no longer exclusively uses wood, materials are all carefully considered as part of a wider regenerative and sustainable mission. "Wood's beauty never goes out of style," Pornpanapong adds. "It remains functional and timeless in the digital age."

CONCEPT
WIT'S COLLECTION
Chiang Mai

Chiang Mai has long been recognised as a mecca for traditional craftsmanship but in recent decades the city has garnered a reputation for combining these skills with canny contemporary design. Wit's Collection executes this balancing act well and owner Wisut Limaree (*pictured*) has been curating a range of handmade creations from craft hotspots including Thailand, Myanmar, China and India since the 1980s. His expertise plays out in a space that feels as much like a gallery as a shop, with treasures in many hues, materials and sizes. There are objects small enough to take home in your luggage, sculptures and even furniture, which can all be shipped internationally.

CONCEPT
AKALIKO
Chiang Mai

Among the many excellent retail establishments in Chiang Mai, Akaliko is unique among them as a champion of minimal contemporary design. The shop is run by writer Arnut Saento and his partner, designer Laudine Dubeaux (*pictured on left, with Saento*), a Thai-French couple who also head up local design studio NAA Design. Akaliko stocks many examples of the duo's work, including bowls, coffee cups, candle holders and vases made from hand-turned teak. The shop itself is beautifully organised, with products arranged in attractive groupings by type, colour or material, making for a very engaging browsing experience.

Craft work
While Akaliko is a showcase for NAA Design's many simple, locally made pieces, products by other Chiang Mai-based designers and makers, including books, clothing, jewellery, homewares and textiles, elevate its offering into a class act of a concept store.

CONCEPT
SPROUT
Koh Phangan

Satika Ozsanay made her name by cooking traditional dishes and spreading regional culinary knowledge when working as a private chef. She has since set up Sprout, a lifestyle shop that allows visitors to dial into the rhythms, flavours, scents and textures of her home in Koh Phangan. Ozsanay lines her wooden shelves – made by a local carpenter – with hand-made products that are all about life's small pleasures. Baby clothes sewn by her mother (*pictured*) can be found alongside hand-poured coconut-wax candles, plant-based skincare products and homemade chilli paste. "Koh Phangan taught me how to live more slowly and intentionally and the shop is a reflection of that," says Ozsanay.

SPECIALIST
CONTAINER
Bangkok

Former architect Kanit Tantiwong applied his meticulous eye for form and function to set up Container, a men's leather accessories label that made an instant mark on Bangkok's retail scene, popping up in top-tier shopping centres. The collection, all handmade locally, is defined by clean lines with very few embellishments; meanwhile other materials, such as nylon, are often incorporated. "I like mixing things up as it gives our bags a more casual vibe," says Tantiwong. The range includes totes, folios, wallets and holdalls – frequent flyers should seek out the C25 Weekender and Berlin L Washbag – with leather from European tanneries and fabrics sourced from Japanese, Korean and Thai producers.

SPECIALIST
CHABATREE
Bangkok

Home and kitchenware brand Chabatree is committed to using Thai wood at its workshop in the country's north. "We love working with Chamchuri wood because it brings a unique warmth and character to each product," says founder Phan Takkavatakarn. He is an engineer by training but a designer at heart, using both to create perfectly weighted cutlery and highly functional salt and pepper grinders. Collaborations with brands from Japan and Germany have extended the range to kettles and cooking pots, though Chamchuri cutting boards and trays are still the bestsellers. "Our customers love them because they're so versatile – not just for food prep and serving, but also for displaying items on countertops," he says.

SPECIALIST
PAÑPURI
Bangkok

Vorravit Siripark was inspired to found Bangkok-based fragrance and skincare company Pañpuri after noticing that Thai spas almost exclusively used foreign products, despite boasting a unique wellness culture. Since its creation in 2003, the brand has become a leading name in the country's luxury skincare and spa-products industry. Pañpuri uses innovative formulas that incorporate botanicals and essential oils in its range of hand creams, face cleansers and perfume oils, combining organic ingredients such as Moroccan rose and Madagascan vanilla with Thai plants including sandalwood, jasmine and lemongrass. Equal care is paid to packaging, with the company using only unbleached paper and environmentally friendly soy ink. The brand is also the driving force behind a pioneering organic spa. For Siripark, the secret to Pañpuri's longevity has been the dedication to creating high-quality products, all made within the country's borders. "We don't really have that many Thai luxury brands," he says. "I want to build a legacy that lasts".

EASTERN GLASS
Bangkok

The oldest working glass manufacturer in the country, Eastern Glass found itself challenged by the slowdown of exports during the coronavirus pandemic. This prompted owner Peerat Chongussayakul (the third generation of his family to head the company) to invest in his home market. He took over a working factory on the outskirts of Bangkok, transforming it into a retail space that showcases both the brand's craftsmanship and its heritage. The original glass-blowing furnace and tools remain on display, offering visitors a glimpse into the artistry behind each piece, all produced with the same skills and techniques used since the 1950s. "It's quite exciting for Thai consumers to see," says Chongussayakul, noting that most locals had never had direct access to the company's wares until now.

SPECIALIST
KORAKOT
Phetchaburi

There are now very few ateliers more aligned with ancient Thai techniques than Korakot Aromdee (*pictured*). As a young boy he learned how to repair and adjust bamboo fishing equipment and knot hemp string into traditional *Chula* kites under the careful instruction of his grandfather in a fishing village in Phetchaburi. His mastering of 12th-century tying techniques and a personal interest in craftsmanship meant that upon graduating from the faculty of decorative arts at Silpakorn University, he was inspired to build up a business focused almost exclusively on *Seesuk* bamboo, a material that he felt hadn't been celebrated enough.

Wicker world
For those looking for a selection of sturdy and beautiful objects, the Korakot brand manufactures large-scale bamboo sculptures, intricate hanging lamps, tray tables, decorative items and swirling light fittings for hotels and exhibitions worldwide.

SPECIALIST
VILA CINI
Chiang Mai

SPECIALIST
SOP MOEI ARTS
Chiang Mai

Even before you enter Vila Cini's shop in the Watgate area of Chiang Mai, you get a sense of the style and sophistication that the company is renowned for. Housed in an elegant refurbished wooden shophouse with arched openings and an abundance of teak, the street presence is the perfect opening gambit for a company that has built a reputation since the 1990s as a purveyor of luxury Thai silk products. Known for its refined adaptations of the traditional Ikat weaving technique, Vila Cini offers a stunning selection of high-end handmade silk items in saturated colourways, including cushion covers, scarves, small bags and purses, clothing and chic, brightly coloured slippers.

Anyone who appreciates a serene atmosphere and luxury handmade goods should make a beeline for Sop Moei Arts. Founder Kent Gregory began fostering connections with the Pwo Karen tribes of the Sop Moei district – a mountainous area of northern Thailand – in the 1970s in a public health capacity. In the 1990s, having observed the weaving skills of the Pwo Karen, he began a collaboration based on the richly coloured textiles that are still at the heart of Sop Moei Arts's offerings. These have since expanded to include baskets, cushions, scarves, handbags and more. Buyers can be assured that every piece is crafted with care and underpinned by meaningful social contributions.

SPECIALIST
DOY DIN DANG POTTERY
Chiang Rai

Arboreal approval
Local materials and native plants are Pantiboon's inspiration – from the area's red clay to bark, seed pods, leaves and flowers. For example, plants are burned and the ash used to create unique glazes. "Wood means rain, wood means air, wood means food and water," Pantiboon says. "Looking after the trees is both a metaphor for my work and my legacy."

Doy Din Dang means "red clay hill", which provides a poetic clue to the work of master potter and artist Somluk Pantiboon (*pictured*). After studying and teaching in Thailand and Japan for more than a decade, Pantiboon returned to Chiang Rai in the early 1990s and bought a plot of land to make pottery by hand. The property is now home to half a dozen buildings, all filled with his work, accompanied by a gallery, shop and café that are open to the public. The shop at Doy Din Dang is filled with all manner of teapots, cups, plates, vessels and vases that demonstrate his enduring commitment to both nature and to simple forms that enhance everyday life.

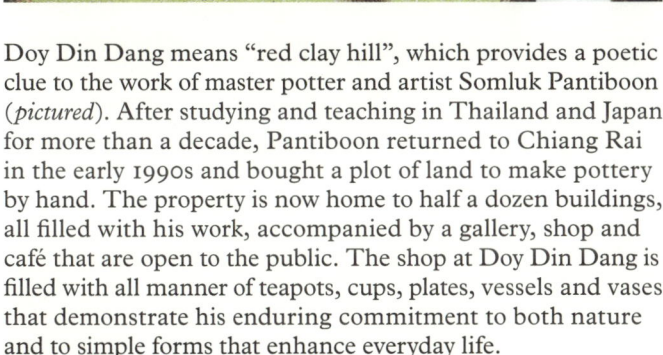

SPECIALIST

SPECIALIST
EARTH & FIRE CERAMICS
Lampang

Earth & Fire Ceramics is the maker of the kind of crockery that you only ever come across in tasteful uptown restaurants – and never quite forget. In fact if you happen to find yourself at Blackitch Artisan Kitchen in Chiang Mai (*see page 60*) you will likely have made personal contact with the company's products. Since 1993, the brand has been crafting an eclectic range of elegant and colourful ceramic pieces. Plates, mugs and bowls all line the shelves of the space that the brand inhabits, hidden away in a small compound set back from the bustle of central Lampang. The multifaceted premises is home to the workshop, factory and studio, as well as a relaxing café, an art gallery and a shop. "Ceramics has always been a reminder of life itself," says Ruiraporn Techathep (*pictured*), creative director and co-founder of Earth & Fire Ceramics. "It's fragile but enduring – simple yet profound." There's a reason why representatives from restaurants all over the country flock to Lampang, each with a vision for their own bespoke tableware.

SPECIALIST
DON MOO DIN
Sakon Nakhon

Don Moo Din – a craft pottery company owned by Walriya Pengsawang (*pictured*) – sells beautiful, natural earthenware that deserves pride of place in anyone's special-occasion-only cabinet. The enormous array of plates, jugs and spoons is treated with natural glazes including ingredients such as ash, feldspar, indigo paste and crushed seashells. Pengsawang maintains her brand's key tenet: injecting identity into every design, while keeping it close to home. "I knew my hobby would one day become my job," she says. "Don Moo is the name of my village and Din means clay. I exclusively use clay from my home town. I find it infinitely inspiring."

Floored genius
After working for a company that designs and weaves carpets for 14 years, Walriya Pengsawang realised that it was time to begin her own journey in 2015. "I knew I wouldn't be able to stay in the carpet business," she says.

NAKAMOL
Phuket

Having found herself with limited funds after moving from Trang to Chicago to pursue a master's degree, student-turned-entrepreneur Sussman Nakamol drew on her love of fashion and developed a jewellery line. While the brand originally took off in the US, Nakamol stayed true to her roots, bringing the business back to southern Thailand and setting up shop in Phuket's Old Town. Inside, her jewellery is displayed in alcoves and draped over vases, as warm light casts soft sparkles. Made using semi-precious stones such as pearl, moonstone and malachite, the collections themselves are timeless. With one foot in the US and the other in Thailand, the designs benefit from an understanding of emerging trends, as well as the refined quality inherent to local craftsmanship.

MALL
EMQUARTIER
Bangkok

As one of the biggest property companies in Bangkok, The Mall Group is the linchpin of the colossal retail development on Sukhumvit Road: the Em District. Building on the concept of Emporium, the city's original luxury shopping destination, The Mall Group unveiled Emquartier in 2015. Designed by New York firm Leeser Architecture, it features seven cinema screens, six storeys of dining terraces, a waterfall and lush gardens. But Kriengsak Tantiphipop, the CEO of Mall Group subsidary The Emporium Group, doesn't call himself a retail developer. "We are building a world of luxury inside Bangkok by embracing nature," he says, gazing up at one of Southeast Asia's largest manmade waterfalls, a masterpiece of green architecture spilling down the exterior of Emquartier. The district was joined by the Emsphere building in 2023. Together, the three Em District shopping malls host more than 1,000 brands and retailers. Dotted among the heavyweights are diverse homegrown heroes such as womenswear line Janesuda.

MALL
SIAM PARAGON
Bangkok

Located in central Bangkok and served by Siam BTS – the busiest station on the Skytrain network – Siam Paragon is a hub for luxury shopping. The plaza contains shops belonging to more than 70 coveted fashion houses, jewellery maisons and watchmakers. Fringed with palm trees and framed by thick windows that filter in the tropical sunshine, Siam Paragon is a cool haven in which to wander – either with purpose or to simply admire the wares on show. If you're not in the mood for shopping, you can catch a film at one of the 13 opulent screens, visit the aquarium or make a beeline for Kinokuniya bookshop. Thailand's supermarkets are best in class, so it's also worth heading to Gourmet Market, where the first customers of the day are greeted with a cheerful *sawasdee*.

MARKET
CHATUCHAK WEEKEND MARKET
Bangkok

It might not be shiny or new but Chatuchak is a permanent fixture on the Bangkok retail scene. With more than 15,000 stalls, it's a sun-baked maze of clothing, crafts, ceramics, furniture, street food, plants and more. The atmosphere is chaotic yet energising and each visit brings fresh discoveries. Sections 2, 3 and 4 stand out for boutique fashion stalls, while sections 5 and 6 hold vintage treasures. Across the road, Bangsue Junction – better known as Red Building Vintage Chatuchak – offers six air-conditioned floors packed with second-hand clothing, antiques and collectables. Public transport is the easiest way to get here and cash is essential.

Market routes
Chatuchak claims to be the largest weekend market in the world, with a site that covers more than 14 hectares and attracts some 200,000 visitors every week. With this big a crowd, parking is obviously a scramble, so public transport is more practical than driving. Catching the BTS to Mo Chit or MRT to Chatuchak Park or Kamphaeng Phet will ensure that you don't spend most of the day in traffic.

MARKET
JING JAI MARKET
Chiang Mai

Chiang Mai is a city of markets. Every weekend, crowds arrive early to root through car-boot sales and buy hill-tribe fabrics. Jing Jai Market to the northeast of the old city offers a more polished and permanent take on the usual jumble of stalls with proper facilities, a selection of shops and an on-site art gallery. Independent clothing brands from around Chiang Mai are the main attraction, alongside a lively farmers' market – ideal for an alfresco breakfast. The site is operated by one of Thailand's largest retail ventures, Central Group, as a platform for small businesses and entrepreneurs. The large Good Goods shop is also worth a visit: it was created to elevate Thai craft and combine traditional techniques with modern design.

Thailand boasts one of the most sophisticated and diverse craft cultures in the world, with a rich history that is inspiring a new generation of contemporary makers. We meet three people shaping the retail and design scene.

MEET THE EXPERTS

RETAILER
SORASAK CHANMANTANA
Onion

Onion is a Bangkok-based clothing retailer created by Sorasak "House" Chanmantana, who began the brand in 2011. Initially online, the company has since moved into the physical world, developing its own products and selling them in-store among its precise selections from around the globe.

How did Onion come to life?
For a time it was no more than a passion project. I was studying music and the business was growing. It became significant enough that I couldn't divide my efforts anymore. We moved into our first shop, which was only a 2 × 4 metre unit, but it was a smart step.

The space is situated away from Bangkok's traditional shopping districts. How has that helped business?
We knew if we were to bring people to our quaint little alleyway, we'd need to accommodate them. We set up our adjoining coffee shop, One Ounce for Onion, which has encouraged people to spend more time here.

Why the name 'Onion'?
Funnily enough, I never eat onions and I ask for them to be removed when I order, so I went for something that would surprise my friends who know I don't touch them. I was nervous about fully committing to the business, so maybe there was an element of confronting fears in there, too.

JEWELLERY DESIGNER
PATCHARAVIPA BODIRATNANGKURA
Patcharavipa

RETAILER
CHNANON SACHDEV
Pronto Original

Jewellery-maker Patcharavipa has gained a cult following for its hand-crafted collections that use rare, precious and unconventional materials, including 18-karat Siam gold and coconut shells. Thanks to founder Patcharavipa Bodiratnangkura's belief that irregularity adds to a product's appeal, each item has an organic appearance.

What is your brand's ethos?
It centres on female empowerment, sustainability and the celebration of artisanal craft. It is also committed to preserving the legacy of Thai jewellery-making, so it blends traditional techniques with contemporary design.

Why is handcraft so important today?
In a world that often prioritises speed over substance, handcrafted items stand as a testament to patience, precision, detail and intention. Each of our pieces tells a story of craft, making it not just an object but a timeless work of art.

What influences your designs?
We're inspired by a blend of architecture, rich cultural diversity and the ever-evolving spheres of art and fashion. We also look at the beauty of different forms and traditions from ancient worlds, where history and craftsmanship converge; we particularly study manmade artefacts and tribal art. Together, these elements create a deep, layered foundation for our design approach.

In the early 2000s, Chnanon Sachdev, founder of Pronto Original, admired the quality of Italian and Japanese denim. He saw an opening for a trendy, international multi-label space in Bangkok, leading him to set up in Siam Square in 2006 – then called Pronto Denim. Today, Pronto Original has seven shops across the city.

What was the initial vision for Pronto Original?
It was simple, in that I wanted a shop that could provide a wide selection of labels that I believed were cool. I also wanted the space to be visually fresh. The experience is like walking into the heart of its owner. But we had to trust that our taste and curation would find success.

Why Siam Square in Bangkok?
Establishing there was a gamble. Back then, there were limited standalone shops but the feel of the area was appealing and there were other young brands like ours taking a punt. Most importantly, we have never left Siam Square, the area where we first launched in 2006. Now it's a major retail hotspot.

What do you consider a perfect retail experience?
Frankly, anything in-person. The social interaction of bricks-and-mortar must be at the forefront. If a well-dressed staff member is giving tips on what looks good, you trust it far better than anything on screen. It's about feeling quality, too. We can list the materials of a product but until you put it on, you never really know.

Whether you're after a bespoke suit, authentic Thai cooking ingredients or some handmade ceramics, there is no shortage of beautiful products to bring home with you. We've scoured the shops, studios and markets to bring you our favourite finds.

THE SHOPPING LIST

I 2 3

1 Doy Din Dang ceramic teapot
  +66 61093 3131
2 Doy Din Dang ceramic teacups
  +66 61093 3131
3 Mowaan traditional Thai
  medicine (*clockwise from top*):
  Hot Formula Medicated Oil;
  Yahom Inthajak Herbal Powdered
  Medicine; Aromatic Refreshing
  Herbal Lozenges
  mowaan.com
4 Hand-stitched silk scarf from
  It's Going Green
  bacc.or.th
5 Kurogin Cacao Spirit
  +66 8156 99445

4 5

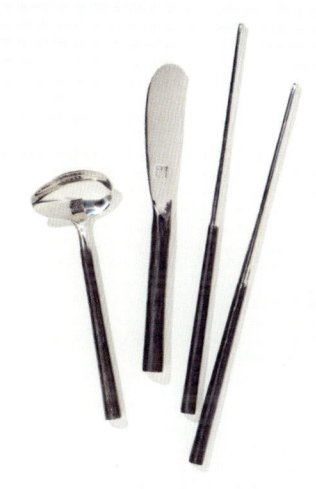

I   2   3

4   5   6

1 Thai Home Industries cutlery
   +66 2234 1736
2 One Night in Bangkok candle
   and The First cleanser by Pañpuri
   panpuri.com
3 Ceramic elephant mug from
   Rachamankha Hotel shop
   rachamankha.com
4 Paz the Dove sculpture from
   Archives Design
   archives-design.com
5 Silk slippers from Vila Cini
   theorientaltextile.com
6 Black cups from Coco Sui Bkk
   bacc.or.th
7 Hin Lad Nai wild honey from
   Sawanbondin Tea House
   +66 81205 3554
8 Taco bag by PDM Brand
   pdmbrand.com

7   8

1 2   3

4   5   6

1 Ceramic jug by Aoon Pottery
   *2, Alley 8, Pathum Khongkha
   Lane, Samphanthawong, Bangkok*
2 Cushion cover from Him Gong
   therayacuratedcollection.com
3 Woven table runner from Thai
   Home Industries
   +66 2234 1736
4 Check-linen Julia tank top by Palit
   palitpalit.myshopify.com
5 Chenille contrast cushion cover
   from Sop Moei Arts
   sopmoeiarts.com
6 Cable knit polo by The Decorum
   shop.thedecorumbkk.com
7 White sugar cane spirit by Aoijai
   Widely available
8 Aluminium cups by Basket Brand
   basketbrandthailand.com

7   8

1 Havana shirt by JBB Menswear
  jbbmenswear.com
2 Siam Breakfast teabags from
  Sawanbondin Tea House
  +66 81205 3554
3 Pumpkin seed *&* cashew nut rice
  crackers by Thaweephan Products
  Widely available
4 Teapot and cup by Siam Celadon
  siamceladon.com
5 Tactile stones by Plan Toys
  th.plantoys.com
6 Thai Monthong Durian crisps by
  Tai Guo Pin
  taiguopin.com
7 Sorghum brushes by Baan Boon
  baanboonbrooms.com
8 Mae Ai First Flush black tea from
  Sawanbondin Teahouse
  +66 81205 3554

1 2

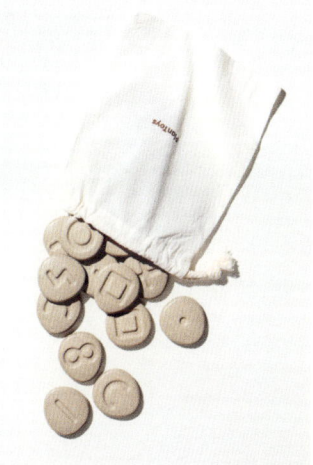

3 4   5

6 7   8

1 2   3

4 5   6

1 Coconut ladle from Siam Celadon
   siamceladon.com
2 Chocolate by Paradai
   939 Rama I Rd, Bangkok
3 Woven rattan hand fans
   Widely available
4 Lemongrass herbal infusion by
   Sawanbondin Tea House
   +66 81205 3554
5 Teak and stoneware cups by Mai
   from Akaliko Design Shop
   akalikodesignshop.com
6 Roasted organic brown rice tea
   by Oyu
   Widely available
7 Wood specimen vases from
   Rivers & Roads
   90 Tha Phae Road, Chiang Mai
8 Wooden Alice bag from Palit
   palitpalit.myshopify.com

7 8

1 Singha soda water
plant.boonrawd.co.th
2 Sunny umbrella by PDM Brand
pdmbrand.com
3 Mosquito incense from
Kalm Village
kalmvillage.com
4 Fabric elephant by Good Goods
central.co.th
5 Siang Pure Oil by Bertram (1958)
bertram1958.com
6 Jun kombucha by Pushers
drinkpushers.com
7 Kao Doi Tea and Araksa Thai
Tea by Araksa
araksatea.com
8 Melon, mango and pineapple
soap by Tai Tier
*Sook Siam, ICON Siam,
Bangkok*

1 2

3 4   5

6 7   8

1 2   3

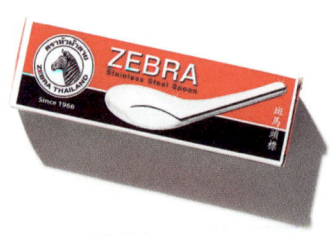

4 5   6

1 Colour-gradation shoulder bag
   by Sop Moei Arts
   sopmoeiarts.com
2 Indigo printed cotton neckerchief
   from Him Gong
   therayacuratedcollection.com
3 Pleated shirt by Long Goy
   +66 89850 5334
4 Jute and sedge woven indigo
   coasters by Maison Craft
   maisoncraft.com
5 Silk sleep mask by Jim Thompson
   jimthompson.com
6 Stainless steel spoons by Zebra
   Widely available
7 Fabric fish decoration from Thai
   Home Industries
   +66 2234 1736
8 Crying Thaiger sriracha sauce
   cryingthaiger.eu

7 8

1   2   3

1 Lip balm by Nuaynard
    nuaynardhandcraft.com
2 Virgin coconut oil by Chaokoh
    tcc-chaokoh.com
3 Brass bell from Thai Home
    Industries
    +66 2234 1736
4 Chocolate by Kad Kokoa
    kadkokoa.co
5 Linen jacket from Rivers & Roads
    90 Tha Phae Road, Chiang Mai
6 Chiang Mai Muse reed diffuser
    by Urban Garden from Rivers
    & Roads
    90 Tha Phae Road, Chiang Mai
7 Hand-dyed socks by Philip Huang
    philiphuang.com
8 Polypropylene woven tote bag
    by Mince
    mincebangkok.com

4   5

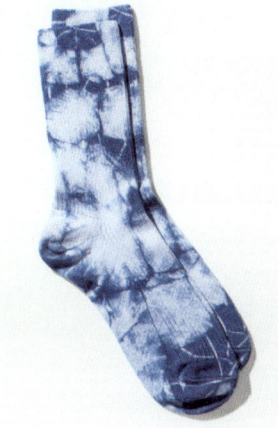

6   7   8

From silk to cinema, via tea, teak and tuk-tuks, Thailand is rich with culture. Here's our rundown of places where you can experience this remarkable heritage – as well as a slew of locations that contribute to the vibrant contemporary scene.

CULTURE

Awe-inspiring temples, gilded statues and intricate shrines are just part of the canvas of modern Thailand. The country is full of creatives with the confidence and curiosity to mix their own rich history – infused for centuries with religion, monarchy, nature and superstition – with external influences. The Thai capital is a hub for the arts. Here, private individuals and organisations lead the way in pushing development around the country. Khao Yai Art Forest, for instance, invites international names to create pieces in situ. The art centre founded by the late Jim Thompson, an American who helped revive the Thai silk industry, is supporting artists from around the region. Then there's the *molam* music of Isan – funky folk beats that get global audiences dancing at the annual Wonderfruit festival. Whether it's through the Muay Thai orchestra's pre-fight *Sarama* music at Rajadamnern Stadium or Buddhist verses sung by the oarsmen of the royal barge procession, this is a nation that moves to its own beat.

THE EDIT

1 Art museums & galleries
Spaces championing Thailand's burgeoning art scene.

2 Culture centres
Multidisciplinary spots playing host to a variety of experiences.

3 Festivals
New Year traditions and music events that draw international crowds.

4 Museums
The best of the nation's repositories.

5 Bookshops
Charming locations dedicated to the written word.

6 Record shops
Explore the sounds of Thailand.

7 Cinemas
A swanky space for the silver screen.

8 Muay Thai arenas & tea plantations
The country's oldest sports venue and tea cultivation history.

9 The experts
Cultural leaders give us their thoughts on Thailand's arts scene.

For details, see pages 216—218.

ART MUSEUM
MUSEUM OF CONTEMPORARY ART
Bangkok

Housing the personal collection of a telecoms tycoon, and run by his son Kanachai "Kit" Bencharongkul, this museum offers a look at Thailand's contemporary art, a lesser known but incredibly rich aspect of its cultural heritage. Presenting pieces from across the country in a light-filled, spacious setting, the museum showcases Thai greats including surrealist artist Prateep Kochabua and stalwarts such as Thawan Duchanee. There are also contemporary responses to traditional Thai arts, with performing arts props, Khon masks and shadow puppets on display, as well as a collection of Western Romantic art on the fifth floor.

Some light in Bangkok
On the outside, the museum appears to be a hulking monolith carved from granite. Its atrium, meanwhile, has a light, breezy feel thanks to windows arranged to resemble jasmine petals. This leads to a pleasing interplay of shadow and sunshine, especially in the summer.

ART MUSEUMS

DISCOVER THAILAND

ART MUSEUM
BANGKOK KUNSTHALLE
Bangkok

The capital's emergence as a leading art hub owes much to the opening of the Bangkok Kunsthalle in 2024. It is both a contemporary gallery and an architectural conservation project. Exhibitions by names such as Yoko Ono and Thai visual artist Korakrit Arunanondchai invite visitors into the lower levels of the venue, which took over a fire-damaged, five-storey former printworks in Chinatown. While lengthy restoration works continue upstairs. Marisa Chearavanont, a prominent art patron, acquired the building to be the sister venue to her Khao Yai Art Forest sculpture park (*see page 133*). Both show works procured from the Giuseppe Panza collection, including sculptures by Richard Nonas and Richard Long, alongside new commissions. "I want to be an art sharer," says Chearavanont.

ART MUSEUM
CHIANG RAI CONTEMPORARY ART MUSEUM
Chiang Rai

Chiang Rai is building a reputation in the creative industry and its Contemporary Art Museum is a principal driver behind this. Bold architecture sets the tone: set among rice fields, the glass-and-steel structure is topped by a pair of towers, each representing one of Chiang Rai's two best-known artists – Thawan Duchanee, who created the Baan Dam Museum (*see page 142*), and Chalermchai Kositpipat, who designed Wat Rong Khun (*see page 160*). Generous double-height spaces host rotating exhibitions showcasing the work of contemporary Thai figures and the café offers stunning views over the surrounding landscape.

ART MUSEUM
MAIIAM
Chiang Mai

Those who take the 30-minute drive out of Chiang Mai will be rewarded on arrival at Maiiam, as they are faced with a two-storey curving plane of mirrored tiles, a bold statement that sets the venue apart. Behind the shimmering exterior is a former warehouse, transformed by Bangkok-based architects Allzone into a future-facing art destination. On display is the collection of art gathered by Jean Michel Beurdeley (a Parisian gallerist who focuses on Thai pieces created since 1995), his late wife, Patsri Bunnag and their son, Eric Bunnag Booth. The venue is a clear indication that the country's contemporary art scene is flourishing and provides a perfect counterpoint to the city's reputation for traditional creative endeavours.

ART MUSEUM
MOLAM BUS
Nakhon Ratchasima

The sight of partygoers dancing on the Molam Bus has become an iconic image of the annual Wonderfruit festival. But this repurposed single-decker is also a mobile exhibition dedicated to the sounds of Isan. Conceived by the Jim Thompson Art Center (*see page 140*), the project began with an as yet unrealised dream to build a permanent museum about Isan culture. The centre staged a three-part exhibition about *molam* at its space in Bangkok and then decided to feature a rotating selection of this show in an old bus. "The nature of modern *molam* is that the musicians and performers don't wait for people, they go to their audience," says Gridthiya Gaweewong, artistic director at Jim Thompson Art Center.

ART MUSEUM
KHAO YAI ART FOREST
Khao Yai

The vast Khao Yai Art Forest is a three-hour drive from its sister institution Bangkok Kunsthalle (*see page 130*), with the pair seen as two sides of the same coin. Here, site-specific commissions are balanced by installations from the permanent collection around the 85-hectare grounds, including Richard Long's "Madrid Circle", an ethereal fog sculpture by Fujiko Nakaya and temporary pieces such as the arachnoid "Maman" by Louise Bourgeois. "Thailand requires a new museum model," says Stefano Rabolli Pansera (*pictured, right*), the institution's founding director. "We are trying to avoid the conventional paradigm."

133

ART GALLERY
NUMTHONG ART SPACE
Bangkok

On a quiet road in residential Ari, this gallery is a magnet for contemporary art lovers in Thailand and beyond, exhibiting local and internationally renowned artists with a strong emphasis on emerging talent. Much of the venue's vision and clarity is attributed to founder Numthong Sae Tang, who has been a longtime champion of making art accessible to the public – he was one of Thailand's very first art dealers and brought his extensive network of artists, collectors and fans together when he opened the gallery in 1997. Exhibitions often showcase cutting-edge installations and envelope-pushing works.

Rising stars
Previous shows at Numthong Art Space have featured Niti Wattuya, Natee Utarit, Kamin Lertchaiprasert and Montien Boonma, known for his conceptual sculptures. It's also well worth taking a moment to browse Tang's personal art library for an insight into his long and varied career.

DHARMA PARK AND INSON WONGSAM ART GALLERY
Lamphun

The son of a temple goldsmith, pioneering Thai artist Inson Wongsam (*pictured*) lived and worked in Paris and New York during the 1960s and 1970s before returning to his hometown of Lamphun, where this private museum, sculpture garden and café is located alongside his home and studio. Wooden buildings in the Lan Na vernacular of northern Thailand house galleries dedicated to the different stages of his long and prolific career. Wongsam has shifted his emphasis this century more towards woodblock prints and large-scale oil paintings, his use of colour becoming more vibrant and radiant with each passing year.

National treasure

Wongsam began as a sculptor, having trained under the legendary art professor Silpa Bhirasri. His abstract works use materials such as teakwood stumps from Thailand and scrap metal from New York to address themes of deforestation and environmental damage. The Thai government appointed him a national artist in 1999 for his work as a sculptor.

CULTURE CENTRE
BANGKOK ART AND CULTURE CENTRE
Bangkok

This art centre is the result of a lengthy campaign by local creatives to have a publicly funded art space. "This challenged commercial encroachment and reasserted the public's right to culture," says the centre's director, Adulaya "Kim" Hoontrakul. It has remained a heavy hitter since debuting in 2008 and the broad roster includes contemporary art from both home and overseas. Among those who have displayed here are Ai Weiwei and multi-disciplinarian Tawee Ratchaneekorn. A programme of talks, film screenings, performances and workshops round out the offering. All this in a building whose soaring atrium and flow of walkways evoke the feel and style of Frank Lloyd Wright's Guggenheim Museum.

CULTURE CENTRE
THAILAND CREATIVE & DESIGN CENTER
Various locations

The Thailand Creative & Design Center (TCDC) is run by a government-funded body and was started in Bangkok in 2005 to support the country's creative talent. Standalone buildings later opened in Chiang Mai (*pictured*), Khon Kaen and Songkhla. Ten smaller outposts, everywhere from Chiang Rai to Phuket, provide a permanent presence in cities across the country. In Bangkok, the agency's 1930s art deco building anchors the annual Bangkok Design Week and the TCDC organises similar events at its other locations. Visitors with work to do can buy a day pass for the price of a cup of coffee and gain access to a design library and other useful resources.

CULTURE CENTRE
KALM VILLAGE
Chiang Mai

Make sure to leave plenty of time to visit Kalm Village – there are at least a couple of hours of boutique browsing and learning about northern Thai craft to be had here. The big draw is the permanent collection of exquisite textiles from different regions of the country, which are displayed either hanging from the ceiling or in vitrines. In the gallery, a rotating programme of exhibitions is shown and, alongside this, no fewer than three lifestyle shops stock an array of beautiful handmade clothing, homewares and jewellery, all of which are designed in-house and made in collaboration with local artisans.

Fabric of the buildings
The village includes nine buildings arranged around two landscaped courtyards. The architecture is unashamedly contemporary with traditional references. The relief brickwork, for example, nods to Thai textiles and basket weaving, and there's a strong use of teak that's been salvaged locally from old houses.

IN FOCUS
FESTIVALS
Let joy be unconfined

Perhaps it's down to the Thai spirit – a love of gathering and finding reasons to celebrate – as to why festivals are an essential part of life here, running from centuries-old traditions to newer events that now draw international crowds. In April, *Songkran*, Thai New Year, turns streets into joyful water fights that are rooted in rituals of cleansing and renewal. Come November, *Loy Krathong* sees lotus-shaped baskets packed with candles and flowers, floating across rivers and lakes as a luminous tribute to water spirits. Further north, in Chiang Mai, *Yi Peng* fills the night sky with thousands of drifting lanterns.

Beyond these classics are some lesser-known regional celebrations such as *Phi Ta Khon* in Loei, a riot of colour in which villagers wear hand-painted masks and take part in parades said to summon protective spirits. More recently, the busy festival calendar has expanded into contemporary culture: Wonderfruit, held annually in Pattaya, has become one of Southeast Asia's leading arts-and-music events, combining live performances with installations and sustainability-driven programming. Boutique gatherings – including jazz, wellness weekends and regional food showcases – continue to emerge, reflecting a country with one foot in the past and the other in the future.

1

1 Traditional dress to celebrate *Songkran*
2 Fearsome *Phi Ta Khon* festival masks
3 Water fights to bring in the new year
4 Fancy fruit offerings
5 *Yi Peng* festival's floating lanterns
6 Molam Bus

2

3

4

Bull rush

The Thai tendency for conviviality has led
to many unusual festivals. One example
is the Chon Buri Buffalo Racing
Festival, which has been highlighting
the bovine icon for more than 150 years.
The normally docile beasts are classed
by weight and can reach up to 50km/h
over a 100-metre course. Less sprightly
animals are welcome in other festival
events, such as the buffalo beauty contest
or the buffalo costume competition.

5   6

MUSEUM
JIM THOMPSON ART CENTER
Bangkok

The artistic director of the Jim Thompson Art Center, Gridthiya Gaweewong, describes its establishment in 2003 as a necessity. At the time, the Jim Thompson House – a popular tourist attraction – was threatened by plans for a new expressway. The art centre was originally inside the museum before moving to a purpose-built home nearby in 2021. Establishing a gallery to promote Thai art and culture helped the case for keeping the site. Now Bangkok's cultural scene is booming and the arts community flocks to the centre for its annual programme of exhibitions featuring marginalised voices and regional artists.

International man of mystery
Jim Thompson was part of the US sailing team at the 1928 Olympic Games and later worked as an interior designer, Second World War spy, hotelier and silk trader. He was a prolific collector of Thai art and, to display his collection, he built the house that bears his name out of five different structures brought from across Thailand. He vanished while on holiday in Malaysia in 1967. His body has never been found.

MUSEUM
THE QUEEN SIRIKIT MUSEUM OF TEXTILES
Bangkok

During her royal tenure – a mantle that she took up in 1950 and served in for 75 years, including periods as Queen, Queen Regent and Queen Mother – Queen Sirikit was celebrated as a style and fashion icon. She had a decades-long collaboration with French designer Pierre Balmain that began in the 1960s with a collection of daywear, evening wear, suits, dress sets and accessories for her six-month tour to 15 western nations. Key pieces can be viewed at the textiles museum that she opened in 2012. Within the venue, located in the Ratsadakorn-Bhibhathana building (formerly the Royal Treasury) inside the grounds of the Grand Palace complex, visitors can discover various galleries, a library and an auditorium when it is open to the public. Highlights from the rotating exhibitions, which change every two to three years, include ceremonial coats richly decorated in metallic thread that were worn by high-ranking male court members and a silk-and-gold-brocade dress by Balmain in the Chakri style, complete with a *sabai* (shoulder cloth) embroidered with sequins and beads.

MUSEUM
THAI FILM ARCHIVE
Nakhon Pathom

Thailand has one of the largest film archives in Southeast Asia, as well as one of the region's most creative film industries. At its purpose-built headquarters, the Thai Film Archive preserves and restores a rich library of newsreels, documentaries, feature films and clips (some freely available on its Youtube channel), while organising a programme of events for visitors. These include temporary exhibitions about famous Thai film-makers, annual festivals and daily screenings at its cinemas of classic Thai pictures and international arthouse releases. "We are called a 'film archive' but we also function like a cinematheque," says deputy director Kong Rithdee, a noted film critic, screenwriter and director.

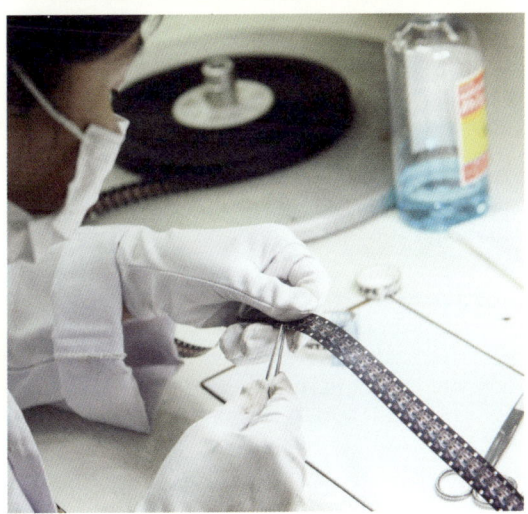

MUSEUM
BAAN DAM MUSEUM
Chiang Rai

Thai artist Thawan Duchanee, a native of Chiang Rai, honed his skills at Silpakorn University, Thailand's most renowned art-education centre. His mature style was heavily influenced by spiritual and mystic themes that are very much in evidence at the Baan Dam Museum. In Thai, *baan* means house and *dam* means black – the moniker refers to the collection of more than 40 mostly black structures that the artist spent more than four decades building and which are dotted around 16 hectares of peaceful parkland. The structures house Duchanee's diverse collection of art and objects, including animal bones, skins and horns.

Dark lands
At first glance, many of the black buildings appear to be traditional Thai architecture but every structure was designed by the artist and built by him and his team. Some structures are strikingly contemporary, resembling concrete bubbles adrift on a sea of lawn. They are even more eyecatching when seen next to one of the resident water buffaloes busily trimming the grass.

BOOKSHOP
OPEN HOUSE
Bangkok

With booksellers increasingly reliant on digital sales, this is a refreshing experience for diehard fans of the printed word. On reaching the top floor of Central Embassy shopping centre, an extensive layout unfolds designed by Tokyo-based design practice Klein Dytham Architecture. Visitors can expect pillars loaded with rare mid-century magazines, two levels of wall-to-wall shelving and a white cuboid-shaped enclosure dedicated to pop-up book and art installations. Chief among the picks are the selections by Hardcover, Open House's independent art bookshop, which largely comprises art and photography monographs and a special section of titles focusing on Asian art and culture. If you take the time to look, you'll find an island solely devoted to issues of Monocle. There's a fine array of dining options too, including a raw bar, should you need a break from browsing. The upper deck features a snaking walkway that curves over the retail-and-restaurant activity below; from here you'll be treated to views of Bangkok through the panoramic windows opposite.

BOOKSHOP
THE BOOKSMITH
Chiang Mai

BOOKSHOP
ASIA BOOKS
Koh Samui

Boasting the title of Thailand's first and largest English-language book retailer and distributor, Asia Books is a magnet for bibliophiles. Founded in 1969, the chain has decades of experience, catering for both local and international tastes. While there are outposts scattered across the country, we recommend visiting Koh Samui's one-of-a-kind, open-air airport to pick up your next new read before jetting off to your next must-hit spot in Thailand. Here you'll find a compact space that's rich in culture, with a tight maze of shelves to guide readers from fiction bestsellers and children's stories to language, lifestyle, business, architecture, travel and design books.

The Booksmith in Chiang Mai's Nimmanhaemin district occupies the ground floor of a shophouse and former art gallery. Proprietor Sirote Jiraprayoon claims that it is the "heart and soul" of his much larger book business. A former executive at national chain Asia Books (*see right*), Jiraprayoon is one of the most influential figures in Thai publishing. His expertise on international publications is sought by libraries and schools, and he also imports English-language books and magazines, supplying large chains and dozens of independent book-shops across Thailand. "We offer underrated books that other shops don't carry, with a focus on art, design and lifestyle imprints," says Jiraprayoon.

BOOKSHOP
SOUL FRIEND & SPIRITUAL GARDEN
Khao Lak

Khao Lak has evolved into Thailand's premier southern wellness hub, with a surf-friendly coastline, national park trails and numerous resorts that embrace holistic living. In this landscape, Soul Friend & Spiritual Garden stands out as Khao Lak's only bookshop and the first New Age meditation studio on the southern coast. Opened in 2022 by Tavisrut Burapat and Chonchaya Burapat, the space was born from a shared passion for mental health. "We wanted to create a place that could support people's wellbeing – not only on their happiest days but also during times of stress or uncertainty," says Chonchaya. Books, they believe, are a lasting tool for sharing knowledge, which is why their curated shelves focus on psychedelic and mindfulness literature in Thai and English. The space extends beyond the bookshop: a meditation studio offers classes in yoga, sound healing and breathwork, while the Listening Café serves Thai cacao hot chocolate, ceremonial-grade matcha, cold-pressed juices and single-origin drip coffee.

RECORD SHOP

ZUDRANGMA RECORDS
Bangkok

Zudrangma Records stocks the best in Thai music. Whether it's funk-influenced *molam* (traditional storytelling) or *luk thung* folk, the shop's broad collection is hand-picked by globe-trotting owner, DJ and musician Maft Sai (*pictured, top right*). Before he makes a decision to buy a record, Maft Sai listens to every track. "If the music isn't good, I won't sell it," he says. The rows of rare finds are shelved ceiling-high. "My customers come from around Bangkok but I also get tourists who are curious about Thai music," he says. "I mostly source from older collectors and those around the world, while some are dead stocks from vinyl produced back in the day."

Top of the shops
While Zudrangma Records is well stocked with new and vintage Thai records, it contains more than just vinyl. The shop also features clothing and recordings on other formats, such as cassettes and 78s. It even issues LPs and CDs on its own label and it also has an online mix channel.

CINEMA
EMBASSY DIPLOMAT SCREENS
Bangkok

The swanky cinema on the top floor of Central Embassy offers a break from the retail rush in the shopping centre below. Each one of the spacious screening rooms is designed to cocoon the audience, whether it's for a drama, thriller, sci-fi or comedy. The RealD XL projection technology and clear-cut surround sound help block off the outside world, allowing for complete immersion into the action in front. Our advice is to book the longest film showing, as you won't want to move from the comforts of your seat once the soft, golden lights dim, the volume is turned right up and the opening credits roll.

Who needs popcorn?
The features at Embassy Diplomat Screens are so sumptuous that they are almost disorientating. Theatre One has a private bar and headphones with language options; in Two and Four guests can recline in business-class-style pods; and Three and Five are flush with daybeds, soft blankets, plumped pillows, mini-bars and butler service.

MUAY THAI ARENA
RAJADAMNERN STADIUM
Bangkok

Known as Muay Thai, Thai boxing or even "the art of eight limbs", this national martial art is an ancient sport that continues to grip audiences across the country and beyond. Rajadamnern Stadium in Bangkok's historic old town is the country's oldest Muay Thai arena and provides a full-on spectator experience. Opening with the *wai kru*, a traditional dance ritual, matches are wild: the sound of the combat fans packing the auditorium can be deafening and the atmosphere electric. Different versions of the sport with shorter or longer bouts feature on different nights of the week. Following an extensive renovation, a state-of-the-art projector was installed, showcasing colourful graphics onto the domed ceiling that often illustrate the history of the sport.

TEA PLANTATION
ARAKSA TEA GARDEN
Chiang Mai

Tea cultivation in and around Chiang Mai has a long history. Chananya "Anne" Phataraprasit stumbled on this industry by accident when she acquired a plot of land with a few overgrown tea plants close to her eco-lodge in 2013 – and research revealed it to be Thailand's first commercial tea plantation. Phataraprasit decided to restart tea production to support the local community while also providing an experience for her guests. The award-winning organic teas are now served in the Thai capital's smartest hotels and exported around the world. The picturesque garden attracts visitors from Chiang Mai, who take a 90-minute drive for lunch or to pick tea and have tastings in the shop.

Thailand is endowed with a rich cultural legacy as well as having one of the most vibrant contemporary arts scenes in Southeast Asia. We meet four people shaping the contours of the nation's creative landscape.

MEET THE EXPERTS

PRATCHAYA "POYSIAN" MAHAPAURAYA & KAVIN THIENVUTICHAI
Sundae Kids

Illustrator Pratchaya "Poysian" Mahapauraya and art director Kavin Thienvutichai, collectively known as the Sundae Kids, have a big following thanks to their comic-style drawings and observations on modern relationships.

What's the status of Bangkok's creative scene?
It has grown a lot in the past decade. We see more galleries, shops and art spaces opening. Because of this, more people are becoming interested in creative work.

How did growing up in Bangkok influence your work?
Since we were little, we were surrounded by media from both the West and the East. We watched Cartoon Network and also read Japanese manga. This mix of influences has shaped our illustration style.

Where do you get your cultural fix in Bangkok?
We are introverts, so we enjoy quiet activities, such as watching films. We also love visiting exhibitions, especially at River City Bangkok. It has a great mix of artists and styles, so there's always something new to see.

What advice would you give to an aspiring illustrator or artist in Thailand?
There's space for everyone in the creative world now. Share your work, stay true to your style and keep going.

PURAT "CHANG" OSATHANUGRAH
Dib Bangkok

KAMOLTHIP "KIM" KIMAREE
Art4d

Purat "Chang" Osathanugrah is the chairman of Dib Bangkok (*see page 153*) and its "little sister" Dib26.

Describe the vibe in Bangkok.
It's a chaotic cultural melting pot that has grown organically to the point where anything goes. Nothing is really zoned or planned here. That's why Thais are so open and fun to be around. The magic happens naturally and the cultural landscape is a reflection of that.

Where does Dib Bangkok fit in?
There has been a bit of a renaissance in the contemporary art scene here. Lots of galleries, art spaces and museums are popping up at the same time, completely unplanned, without any publicly funded incentive whatsoever. Every great city deserves a great museum and we want Dib Bangkok to be that institution for contemporary art.

Where do you get your cultural fix in Bangkok?
Music is a big part of my family and I consider myself to be a bit of a moonlighting musician. I can play anything in a rock band and I'll pretend that I play saxophone. A decade ago you could only pick a handful of jazz bars but now there are so many places. Buddha & Pals is a funky spot.

You have brought music into Dib. Tell us more about that.
Contemporary art also means contemporary culture and you can't have that much fun without music. Our sister venue Dib26 is more of a multidisciplinary space for exploration, discovery and play within the creative arts as a whole. That can be music or design or it could also be vintage furniture and education.

A prominent voice in the Southeast Asian design and architecture community, Kamolthip "Kim" Kimaree began her career as a designer before taking on her role as the managing director of *Art4d*.

What does 'Art4d' do differently from other publications?
After trying to keep up with the fast-paced world of social media, we realised that some things just aren't our strong suit, so we stepped back a bit and did what we believed was right. We can't compete with quantity but we can create quality. We discovered that the niche market remains viable, so we transformed our monthly magazine into a collectable, timeless monograph tailored to readers' needs.

What qualities make for a successful publication?
It's about how well it captures the spirit of the story using creativity and criticism. Each publication should leave some questions rather than just offer answers; it should spark conversation in a productive way.

What is the future of print media?
I assume that it will become a collectable object, similar to records and photo negatives, which convey a sense of art and aesthetic from particular perspectives.

What are your thoughts on Thailand's media landscape?
It has undergone significant changes following the emergence of social media and streaming platforms, both of which pose intense competition. The speed and volume of content are key factors for consideration and the industry needs to understand how to optimise both to ensure algorithm success and to limit the decline of traditional outlets.

The architecture of Thailand is a major part of the country's cultural legacy. Influenced by the tropical climate, religious beliefs and locally available materials, there is an extraordinary richness and variety – from ancient temples to high-rise towers.

ARCHITECTURE

The story of Thai architecture is a long and illustrious one, dating back more than 1,000 years and absorbing influences from China, the Khmer Empire and India along the way. The enduring image is of enchanting temples with curved roofs, gold spires and intricate decorations that can still be seen in abundance throughout the land. But as you will see in the following pages, architecture in Thailand is more than just temples. Everything from houses to restaurants, palaces and even banks reflect the country's culture, religion, climate and way of life. We'll take you to spectacular brick and stone ruins from the 14th century and a 20th-century teak palace from the Kingdom of Siam. Thailand also has a lot to offer in the way of contemporary architecture, with a roster of local talent and international design practices contributing formidable additions to Bangkok's built heritage, as well as some of the 21st century's most striking sacred spaces, continuing the cycle of influence between the past and the present.

THE EDIT

1 **Dib Bangkok**
Architectural landmark for contemporary art.

2 **Mahanakhon**
Pixel-perfect high-rise on Bangkok's skyline.

3 **Nai Lert Park Heritage Home**
A teak house for an entrepreneurial explorer in the heart of Bangkok.

4 **Thai mid-century modernism**
Concrete cool in the post-war boom.

5 **Central World**
Through the arched windows, a retail fantasy awaits.

6 **Ayutthaya Historical Park**
Atmospheric 14th-century ruins.

7 **Wat Rong Khun**
A glittering Buddhist temple by a visionary artist.

8 **Wat Santi Wanaram**
Lotus flower-shaped temple on a lake.

9 **Maruekhathaiyawan Palace**
Spacious former royal seaside residence.

10 **Sino-Portuguese shophouses**
Candy-hued architectural confectionery.

DIB BANGKOK
Bangkok

In a former steel warehouse near the port area of Bangkok, Dib, which means "raw" or "authentic" in Thai, houses more than 1,000 artworks acquired over 40 years by collector Petch Osathanugrah. Thai architect Kulapat Yantrasast of Why Architecture transformed the 1980s building into an enclosed compound with a central courtyard, featuring a tranquil pool and The Chapel, a cone-shaped gallery space. At Dib Bangkok, the journey starts on the ground level with its industrial aesthetic, while the second level is more intimate and the third houses high-ceilinged galleries illuminated by natural light from skylights in a dramatic saw-tooth roof.

MAHANAKHON
Bangkok

The Mahanakhon, by Büro Ole Scheeren, cuts a dash on Bangkok's skyline. A 3D ribbon of architectural pixels twists around the structure and the resulting protrusions and indentations create space for terraces, plunge pools and floating glass rooms, all with spectacular views for those in the 200 luxury apartments that occupy most of the floors. Elsewhere in the building, The Standard hotel is a fine addition to the Silom district's drink-dine-stay offerings, complete with an outdoor bar terrace. To literally top it all off, the Skywalk rooftop and observatory offers safety-first daredevils a chance to take to the "glass tray" on the 78th floor, 310 metres above Bangkok's streets.

HERITAGE HOUSE
NAI LERT PARK HERITAGE HOME
Bangkok

Entrepreneur, philanthropist, explorer, collector, property developer: Lert Sresthaputra was a singular character who left behind an unparalleled architectural legacy in Bangkok. Having acquired land along the Saen Saep canal in what is now downtown Sukhumvit, he built a family home in 1915 that includes many traditional Thai details in its teak-framed bungalow form, including three-tiered roofs. A series of interconnected indoor and outdoor spaces are protected from monsoon rains by deep overhanging eaves. A trove of original furniture and antiques are beautifully arranged throughout, warranting at least an hour of browsing.

VARIOUS
THAI MID-CENTURY MODERNISM
Bangkok

1

2 3

1 Krung Thai bank, 1970
2 Sarasin building, 1968
3 Chamnan Overseas Trade HQ, 1970s
4 Indra Regent Hotel, 1970
5 Embassy of India, 1980
6 Boonnumsup House, 1979

4

5

6

It is easy to spot Thailand's distinct brand of mid-century modernism. In the 1960s and 1970s a post-war economic boom saw rapid urban expansion occur, leading to the sculptural aesthetics and optimistic spirit of mid-century modernism being applied to all kinds of buildings. This adoption of the style was bolstered by US-educated Thai architects bringing modernist principles home with them and adapting them to the tropical climate. Utilising novel thin-shell concrete technology, these architects created sculptural façades featuring arches, scallops, ribs and grids – always in striking pure white – that protected the glass behind them from the sun and monsoon rains.

SHOPPING CENTRE
CENTRAL WORLD
Bangkok

International architecture practice Linehouse brings a welcome dose of understated elegance to downtown Bangkok, right in the middle of the city. Amid the glitz and glass, traffic and towers of Pathum Wan, the two-layered façade of the Central World shopping centre offers a gently shifting rhythm of overlapping arches in a variety of heights and widths. The outer layer of pale grey, ribbed concrete provides a unifying container for the seven floors of retail, food and entertainment offerings within, while a second layer in dark grey appears to slip and slide beneath the outer layer, bringing light in, and views out, of the spaces inside.

ARCHAEOLOGICAL SITE
AYUTTHAYA HISTORICAL PARK
Ayutthaya

The old city of Ayutthaya dates from about 1350 and flourished as the second capital of the Kingdom of Siam for more than 400 years. It was later destroyed by the Burmese army in 1767, after which it was abandoned. The ruins, now a protected Unesco site, include hundreds of important archaeological areas, among them dozens of Buddhist temples. The iconic stone reliquary towers (or *prangs*) are an atmospheric reminder of a once-thriving city that was, in its heyday, one of the most cosmopolitan and influential in the world. Ayutthaya is 80km north of Bangkok and can be visited as an easy day trip from the capital.

TEMPLE
WAT RONG KHUN
Chiang Rai

Artist Chalermchai Kositpipat, who gained a reputation in the 1980s and 1990s for paintings and murals that reinterpreted Buddhist themes in a contemporary way, was inspired to devote the rest of his life to the creation of what he dreamed would be "the most beautiful temple in the world – in my own style". Work started in 1997, and the structure is now part of a complex encompassing multiple buildings and gardens. The all-white form makes a beguiling sight, glittering thanks to pieces of mirrored glass embedded in its surfaces. Kositpipat still works at the site regularly, supervising repairs and improvements that he anticipates will take many decades to complete.

WAT SANTI WANARAM
Udon Thani

In the far northeastern corner of Thailand stands Wat Santi Wanaram (also known as the White Lotus Temple). Completed in 2019, the temple is a newer addition to the country's architectural legacy, a heritage that stretches back more than 1,000 years and includes more than 40,000 Buddhist temples (or wats). The structure appears to float on the calm waters of lake Nong Nam Esan Keaw, its 24 petals enclosing a circular space that features scenes from the Buddha's life. Aside from drawing admiring visitors, the site is also a meditation space for practising monks and local school students, who attend meditation-practice camps.

PALACE
MARUEKHATHAIYAWAN PALACE
Cha-am

Ercole Manfredi moved to Thailand in 1909, one of many Italian architects employed in the last decades of the Kingdom of Siam. From 1912, he worked in the Ministry of the Royal Household with King Vajiravudh and the Maruekhathaiyawan Palace is an expression of his dual cultural influences. Initial sketches were drawn by the king, then developed and executed by Manfredi, with the project completed in 1924. The result is a blend of Thai and Italian traditions, with 16 teak buildings connected by balconies, verandas and staircases, all elevated in the Thai manner to protect from flooding and promote ventilation. Its detailing and decoration, meanwhile, demonstrate Italian flair.

SHOPHOUSES
SINO-PORTUGUESE SHOPHOUSES
Phuket

It's difficult to resist the charms of the candy-coloured, richly decorated shophouses that are so synonymous with Phuket. They also represent a fascinating history that dates back to the early 1500s, when the area's Portuguese merchants often employed Chinese labourers to build these structures (typically a two-storey property with a shop on the ground floor and a residence above). The result was a hybrid style, featuring colourful tiles, elaborate stuccowork and wooden latticework, with some finished with exquisite gold detailing. Take a walk down Soi Romanee, in Phuket's Old Town, for some of the best examples of these beautifully restored historic landmarks.

With about 3,200km of coastline, in excess of 1,400 islands and with more than a quarter of the kingdom devoted to national parks and wildlife sanctuaries, Thailand has a wealth of natural spots to tempt you outdoors.

THE GREAT OUTDOORS

Whether you're a swimmer, a hiker or a climber, Thailand has an abundance of outstanding natural locations for lovers of the outdoors. There is no shortage of activities to try or spectacular spots in which to enjoy them and thanks to daytime temperatures that rarely dip below 30C, they can be enjoyed throughout the year. Mountains cover much of northern Thailand, where dreamy mist threads through the valleys at sunrise and remote waterfalls cascade in thunderous curtains. In the south, island and water-based activities reign supreme. Beaches, bays, inlets, coastal caves and coral seas offer some of the best snorkelling, scuba diving and kayaking in the world. Because of the tropical climate there's an abundance of wildlife, including exotic fish, reptiles and birds. Larger beasts, including elephants, water buffalo and deer, can be glimpsed in the mountains and plains further north. So pack a towel, some comfy footwear and a pair of binoculars – it's time to explore.

THE EDIT

1 **Beaches**
Six secluded spots that flaunt the natural beauty Thailand is famed for.

2 **Marinas**
A luxury lifestyle hub decked out with sleek sailboats and a sailing club.

3 **National parks**
Breathtaking rainforests, mangroves, caves, hiking trails, snorkelling spots and dive sites.

4 **Monasteries**
A rustic Buddhist monastery that spirals around a towering sandstone outcrop.

5 **Rice terraces**
A river valley that showcases Thailand's mountainside agricultural practices.

BEACH
BOTTLE BEACH
Koh Phangan

Reached by long-tail boat from Ban Chaloklum or via a jungle trail over palm-studded ridges, Bottle Beach (Hat Khuat) is one of Koh Phangan's more relaxed hideaways. Its broad crescent of powdery white sand eases gently into turquoise water that stays calm most of the year – perfect for long swims or kayaking to hidden coves. Breezy, open-air dining spots serve grilled fresh fish, curries and cold beer. As dusk falls, waves hush the shoreline in place of the pounding bass found on other beaches, creating a rare tranquillity. Visit between December and April for smooth seas, clear skies and easy boat access. Bring mosquito repellent and cash – there are no ATMs here.

BEACH
LIPA NOI
Koh Samui

On Koh Samui's less-developed west coast, Lipa Noi stretches along a wide swath of pale sand and coconut palms. Far from Chaweng's nightlife, the area offers a slower pace with a handful of beachfront cafés, family-run guesthouses and discreet boutique villas. Sunsets can be spectacular, painting the horizon gold and crimson, with Ang Thong National Park's islands silhouetted in the background. The rock-free shallow water here makes it one of the safest beaches. An inland road meanders past coconut groves, small temples and markets where locals shop. Evenings are quiet, though weekend gatherings sometimes bring bonfires and acoustic guitars. Natural shade is limited, so bring an umbrella or beach tent.

BEACH
TANOTE BAY
Koh Tao

Tucked into Koh Tao's rugged east coast, Tanote Bay is a deep, steep-sided cove with excellent snorkelling. Coarse golden sand meets water that drops to a coral reef alive with parrotfish, butterflyfish and hawksbill turtles. A huge boulder in the middle of the bay provides a diving platform for the adventurous. Hillside bungalow resorts offer sunrise views, while evenings are relaxed, with simple Thai restaurants under string lights and the sound of geckos. Getting here means navigating a winding forest road, which deters casual visitors, but the reward is a scenic and quiet bay perfect for those who like beaches with a sense of discovery.

BEACH
RAILAY BEACH
Krabi

Railay Beach is one of Krabi's most striking coastal spots. Less a single beach than a compact peninsula that feels like an island, Railay Beach is accessible only by boat, thanks to the cliffs that separate it from the mainland. It rose to prominence in the 1980s when climbers discovered its limestone walls but those who don't climb can still enjoy adventures such as swimming, kayaking or visiting Phra Nang cave, where a shrine to the spirit of a drowned princess blends local legend with everyday life.

BEACH
PAKARANG BEACH
Phang Nga

Named after the Thai word for the coral fragments that are sometimes washed ashore, Pakarang Beach is a peaceful, golden stretch at the north end of Khao Lak. Casuarina trees fringe the shore and low tide reveals sandbars that stretch toward the horizon. With no beach clubs or jet skis, Pakarang suits those seeking tranquillity. Local seafood shacks beside the sand grill the day's catch and even in high season, the beach feels uncrowded. Sunsets here are cinematic, with deep reds melting into violet over the Andaman Sea and migrating birds appearing between November and February. The beach is great for long solitary walks but wear light footwear if exploring at low tide because of the broken coral.

BEACH
YANUI BEACH
Phuket

Yanui Beach is a pocket-sized crescent of soft white sand framed by rocky headlands that shelter calm, clear water. Though small, the cove attracts a lively mix of families, anglers and travellers, offering a quieter alternative to Phuket's big-name beaches. At low tide, natural rock pools emerge, perfect for children and curious wanderers to peer into to spot crabs and darting fish. Vendors on the road opposite the beach keep things casual, renting snorkel gear and kayaks and selling fruit shakes, cold beer, coconuts and snacks under tattered umbrellas. Scenic clifftop viewpoints are just minutes away, where sunsets spill across the Andaman without Patong's crowds. Arrive early to enjoy the more tranquil morning hours.

MARINAS

ROYAL PHUKET MARINA & PHUKET BOAT LAGOON

Phuket

Just a few minutes apart on Phuket's east coast, these two marinas cater to quite different nautical tribes. Royal Phuket Marina is the glossy relative newcomer, built in the mid-2000s as a luxury lifestyle hub. Sleek boats line its sheltered basin, while quayside promenades host fine restaurants, wine bars, boutique shops and spas. Upscale condos and villas complete the scene. By contrast, Phuket Boat Lagoon – opened in the 1990s – is more down-to-earth. Its focus is on functionality: a full-service boatyard, dry dock, chandleries and modest restaurants frequented by sailors, families and long-term liveaboards. Apartments, a hotel and local shops lend it the air of a small village.

NATIONAL PARK
KHAO SAM ROI YOT NATIONAL PARK
Prachuap Khiri Khan

An hour south of Hua Hin, the road slips past sleepy fishing villages and pineapple fields before the outline of Khao Sam Roi Yot National Park appears on the horizon. The name of Thailand's first coastal national park translates to "Mountains of 300 Peaks" and it's obvious why. Khao Sam Roi Yot's limestone cliffs rise from a patchwork of wetlands, mangroves and beaches. The hike to Phraya Nakhon Cave takes 45 minutes, climbing through forest before opening into a chamber where sunlight streams onto the Kuha Karuhas Pavilion – built for King Rama V in 1890. Other activities include birdwatching, kayaking and spotting dusky langurs. End the day on Laem Sala Beach, then return to Hua Hin for a seafood feast.

MARINAS & NATIONAL PARKS

DISCOVER THAILAND

NATIONAL PARK
KHLONG LAN NATIONAL PARK
Kamphaeng Phet

This little-known national park feels like a forgotten world tucked into Kamphaeng Phet's northern area. At its heart thunders Khlong Lan Waterfall, a 100-metre cascade that fans out across a cliff before tumbling into a swimmable basin – a natural amphitheatre of echo and spray. Trails thread upward through tropical forest alive with hornbills, langurs and the occasional muntjac, rewarding hikers with cool breezes and sudden vistas over rice valleys far below. The villages at the park's edge still practise old ways of life – bamboo fish traps in creeks and betelnut chews traded at tiny shops serve as reminders that not all of Thailand has been remade for tourists.

NATIONAL PARK

TARUTAO NATIONAL MARINE PARK
Satun

Koh Tarutao, the largest island in Tarutao National Marine Park, offers a rugged escape of empty beaches, rainforest and wildlife. A prison camp from 1938 to 1948, Tarutao now draws nature lovers. The island's blend of history, nature and solitude rewards those willing to travel a little further. Park-run bungalows and campsites – the only accommodation available – offer a secluded setting. Bring essentials, including cash, food, water and mosquito repellent, because there are no ATMs or shops. Boats to Tarutao depart from Pak Bara pier during the high tourist season but the park closes from 16 May to 30 September because of intense winds and heavy rainfall, as well as to allow for marine rehabilitation.

NATIONAL PARK

SIMILAN ISLANDS NATIONAL PARK
Phang Nga

Strung like gems across the Andaman Sea, the Similan Islands are Thailand's marine crown. This protected archipelago is known for its healthy coral reefs, granite boulders tumbling into turquoise water and powdery white beaches. On land, thick tropical forest covers much of the islands, sheltering birdlife and monitor lizards. Underwater, though, is the main draw of the site: crystal-clear water reveals gardens of hard and soft coral, schools of batfish and parrotfish, graceful turtles and, with luck, manta rays or a passing whale shark. Drift dives over massive boulder formations feel otherworldly, while shallow reefs brim with smaller wonders. The park is open from October to May, with boats departing from Khao Lak.

THE SURIN ISLANDS
Phang Nga

Off Thailand's west coast, Mu Koh Surin National Park is Thailand's most unspoiled archipelago. Accessible for just six months per year and covered in primary rainforest teeming with wildlife – including rare mouse deer, giant fruit bats and eagles – the five islands are home to an indigenous Moken community. Chong Khat on Koh Surin Nuea offers bungalow accommodation and serves as a nesting ground for sea turtles, while snorkellers can spot all manner of colourful reef fish and even rays and sharks.

NATIONAL PARK
KHAO SOK NATIONAL PARK
Surat Thani

Encompassing one of the world's oldest rainforests, Khao Sok is the stuff of jungle dreams – primaeval foliage cloaking limestone pinnacles that pierce the sky like green fangs. At its centre lies Cheow Lan Lake, a huge reservoir dotted with raft-house lodges where dawn mists float over mirror-like water, longtail boats nose between karst towers streaked with orchids and gibbons call across the canopy. Trekking trails lead deep into bamboo groves, with caves hiding ancient stalactites. Despite its popularity, Khao Sok still feels wild, especially beyond the main trails. Storms lend the landscape a wilder, more cinematic edge but bring leech protection in the rainy season.

MONASTERY
WAT PHU THOK
Bueng Kan

Wat Phu Thok is a remote monastery that spirals around a sandstone outcrop, with seven levels of wooden stairways clinging to sheer cliffs, each symbolising a different stage of Buddhist enlightenment. As you make the strenuous climb, each level feels cooler than the one before. Built in the 1960s, it remains an active monastery. The exposed walkways can be vertigo-inducing but the views are worth the effort. Visit between November and February for clear skies and pleasant temperatures.

RICE TERRACES
PING RIVER VALLEY
Chiang Mai

While some plucky Chiang Mai residents take to the Ping river in the city atop paddle boards or in kayaks, it's more rewarding to head out of the city and follow the valley into the hills of northern Thailand. The Ping meanders through the suburbs but it's not until it shakes the city off its banks that its true green beauty is revealed. Highway 107 snakes alongside the river through a lush valley, as you head into Chiang Dao and beyond, towards the small town of Fang and on to Chiang Rai. Switching to Highway 1178 sticks closer to the Ping and takes you deeper into rural hamlets and open countryside. You will also spot terraced rice paddies, as well as pineapple and tea plantations.

PART 02

PUT DOWN ROOTS

So you're considering staying a little longer, perhaps even making Thailand home? We've visited the neighbourhoods to invest in, found the architects and designers to commission and met a few people who've already made the move.

With a tropical climate, jaw-dropping landscapes and incredible food, Thailand offers an enviable quality of life and plenty of opportunities for the entrepreneurially inclined. Here are our suggestions for where to put down roots.

WHERE TO LIVE

ARI
Bangkok

Popular among the wealthy, this leafy, residential neighbourhood in
north-central Bangkok is desirable for its trendy dining spots, expansive
retail offering, leading art scene and buoyant economy.

Closest airport: Don Mueang
International is a 20-minute drive away
Eat: Khua Ling Pak Sod
Drink: Yellow Lane
Shop: The Decorum
Do: Numthong Gallery

Bangkok continues to dominate commercial, cultural
and political life in Thailand, making it the clear choice
for most new arrivals. European and Japanese expats
tend to congregate in modern apartments around
the lively Sukhumvit Road offshoots, but those in
search of a leafier, more residential area (as well as the
opportunity to live in a standalone family house with a
garden) eventually discover Ari. Once a sleepy enclave
for retired officials and affluent businesspeople, it is
now brimming with independent restaurants, cafés,
hotels, street-level retail, kickboxing gyms, galleries,
theatres and schools. It is also home to a surprising
mix of corporate headquarters, central-government
departments, Thai political parties and international
NGOs, all of which mean reliable weekday foot traffic
before the off-duty crowd arrives on Saturdays and
Sundays. Downtown Bangkok is directly accessible
using the Skytrain, and Don Mueang International
Airport is a 20-minute drive away. Most importantly,
Ari never floods during the rainy season.

NEIGHBOURHOOD
NIMMANHAEMIN
Chiang Mai

Those seeking an urban buzz outside of Bangkok choose
Nimmanhaemin for its flavourful cuisine, thriving nightlife
and plentiful business opportunities.

Closest airport: Chiang Mai
International is a 15-minute drive away
Eat: Huen Phen
Drink: Ristr8to
Shop: Palit
Do: Gallery Seescape

While Chiang Mai's suburbs of Mae Rim, Hang Dong and Doi Saket attract clusters of expats who like greenery on their doorstep, those who want to be in the heart of the city choose Nimmanhaemin Road. The narrow, odd-numbered lanes can sometimes make addresses difficult to find but lend themselves to spontaneous exploration. The walkable grid teems with local craft shops, massage studios, almost too many eating options – including the rustic Ginger Farm Kitchen and the Japanese-Thai dishes of Blackitch Artisan Kitchen (*see page 60*) – and

the serious caffeine roasters of Ristr8to. At the northern end of the main road, shopping centre One Nimman evokes a summery European piazza, blending indoor and outdoor with regular pop-up markets and a handful of interesting dining options drawing high-season crowds. Across the junction is Think Park; its mostly open-air eateries draw a younger, more local clientele. The road's popularity means that traffic can build up so it makes sense to go fully local and opt for two wheels over four to get around.

ISLAND
KOH SAMUI
Surat Thani

A top choice for relaxed island living, Koh Samui is known for its picturesque scenery and laidback lifestyle, both of which lure a vibrant expat community.

Closest airport: Samui International Airport is 2km north of Chaweng
Eat: Tree Tops Signature Dining
Drink: House of Suzy
Shop: Asia Books
Do: Lipa Noi beach

Phuket's pacy development into a fully fledged city has seen Koh Samui – Thailand's second-largest island – become the nation's top choice for tropical-island living. Residents talk proudly of their home's laidback lifestyle and it's hard to spot a building higher than four storeys. Hospitality is the dominant industry and the island is an incubator for independent ventures. Australian chef Leandro Panza arrived in 2016 after quitting his job in Melbourne. "I was done with it," he says from the sandy shores around 2 Fishes, his seafood restaurant, which celebrates the local catch. Similarly, New Zealander William Norbert-Munns (*see page 84*) relocated his family from Cambodia to Lamai, a popular expat neighbourhood on the island's southeast coast, for some fresh air and restorative walks along the beach. Bangkok Airways owns Koh Samui's airport and operates almost every flight to and from the island. Ticket prices for tourists are relatively high but residents get special rates and seem rather content with the arrangement.

185

PINAREE SANPITAK
Bangkok

Thailand's broad spread of architectural influences has resulted in some innovative accommodation. One striking example is this spacious, airy home studio in urban Bangkok.

Artist Pinaree Sanpitak can see all of Bangkok's urban canvas – the shophouses, the food markets and the twisted, pixelated form of the gleaming Mahanakhon (*see page 154*) – from the top floor of her four-storey house in a quiet Sathorn alley. The purpose-built "studio home" was designed by Allzone founder Rachaporn Choochuey. "The challenge for the architect was that I don't get up in the morning and leave for work," says Sanpitak. "I'm here 24/7, moving around the house, cooking, gardening and working." Sanpitak is a leading Thai contemporary artist and her mix of painting, sculpture and installation features in art fairs and exhibitions around the world. Her main studio is two storeys high: it starts on the second floor to benefit from the light from the floor-to-ceiling windows and opens out to allow the delivery of large canvases. One of two smaller studios upstairs is where her son Shone Puipia began his fashion label. Mother, son and grandma live on the same compound and Shone and his team come over on work days. "We are always exchanging ideas and we collaborate a lot," says Sanpitak.

RESIDENCE
NAKORNSANG STUDIO
Bangkok

Working from home can lead to all kinds of compromises,
not least if your job is creating wooden furniture. Yet blending work
and living spaces harmoniously under such circumstances is possible,
as this handsome home shows.

Nakornsang Studio, set on a quiet residential lane north of Chatuchak Market (*see page 116*), is both a home and a family-run workshop that acts as a live archive of fine woodworking. The main house, a modern structure where company founder Charnon Nakornsang lives with his wife and daughter, is pared back so focus is on the pieces within. Chairs, tables, stairs and even railings are conceived as sculptures that are functional yet expressive. "[They're] designed to shape the atmosphere as much as to serve daily life," says Nakornsang.

What began with a small set of hand tools has since grown into a furniture brand rooted in meticulous woodworking that merits detailed inspection. "I want my work to be the kind that invites you to look closer. It's the proportion and the details that really stand out," adds Nakornsang. Across the garden, the workshop hums with experimentation, with new creations taking shape before finding a place in the showroom-home. The effect is an intimate portrait of a maker's life, where craft and the everyday exist together.

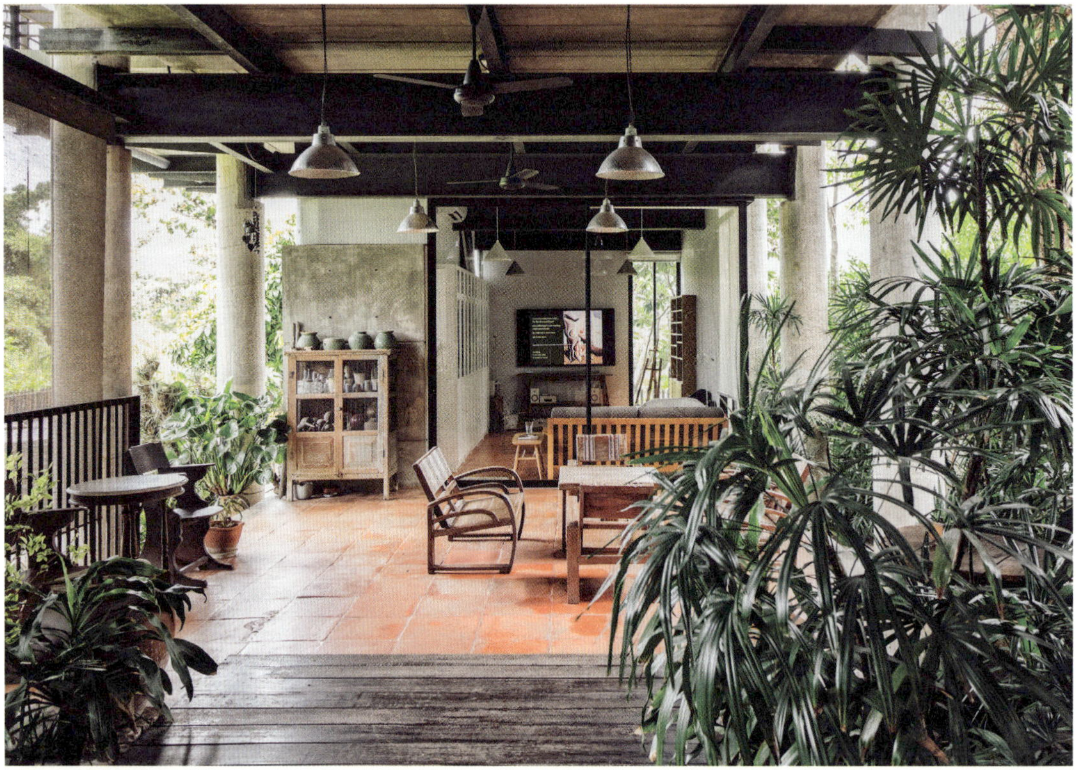

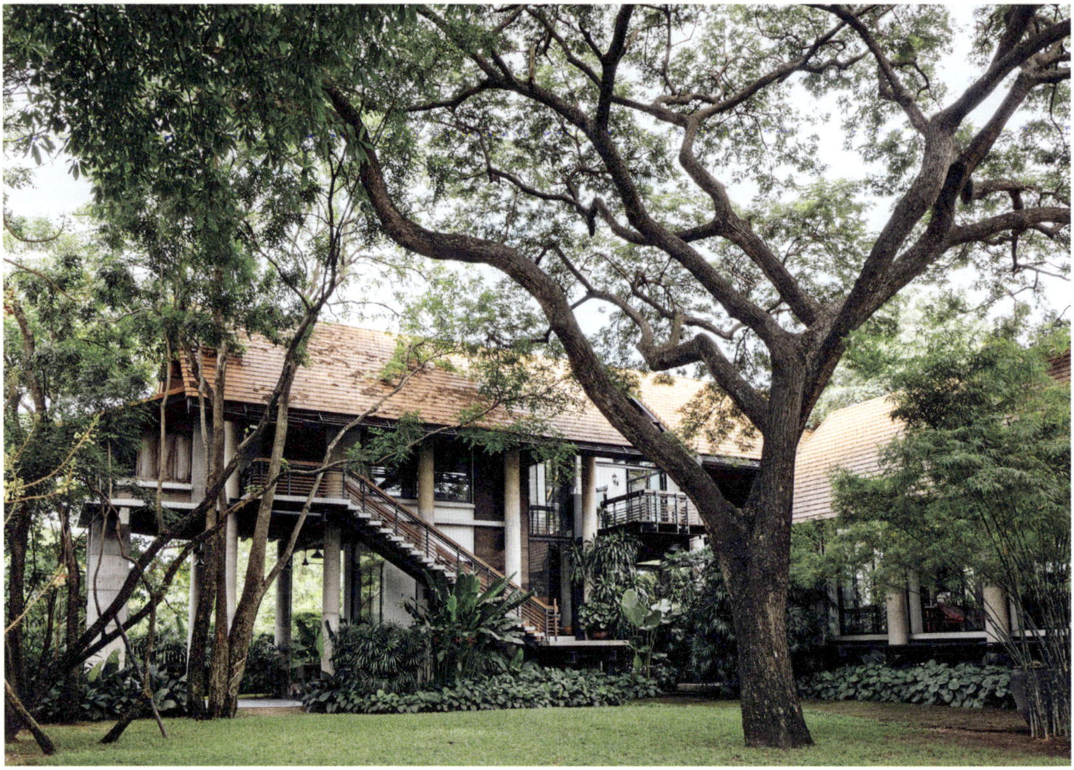

RESIDENCE
PIRAST PACHARASWATE
Bangkok

Thailand's tropical climate poses unique challenges for architects but one expert in tropical modernism decided to put his theories to the test. The result was a home built using modern techniques and materials that coexists perfectly with its surroundings.

Architect Pirast Pacharaswate acquired land in Thonburi to build his own house not long after moving back home from the US with a master's degree. He was lecturing on tropical modernism at Bangkok's Chulalongkorn University at the time and wanted to put his ideas into practice. "Designing and building my own house made teaching architecture easier," says Pacharaswate, who grew up in Thonburi. He fell in love with an overgrown plot covered in coconut and banana trees, and wasted no time turning his ideas into a design, completing East

House in 2001. Pacharaswate wanted to create climate-responsive architecture in Thailand, making use of modern technology and durable materials. To maximise space for a large garden and the umbrella-like canopy of a mature rain tree he planted as a sapling more than two decades ago, he positioned the one-bedroom home, study and open-sided pavilion, or *sala*, in the northwest corner of the 1,600 sq m plot. The T-shaped house, which is elevated to escape the moisture, is split into two buildings, one taller than the other to provide afternoon shade.

We introduce you to some of our most trusted architects and designers. These creatives can fit out a condo in the capital, furnish a boutique hotel or sketch a concept for a commercial art gallery. For contact details, see pages 216—218.

ARCHITECTURE & DESIGN

ARCHITECTURE STUDIO
ONION
Bangkok

Arisara Chaktranon and Siriyot Chaiamnuay (*pictured, on left, with Chaktranon*), Onion's co-founders, met at the prestigious Chulalongkorn University in Bangkok in the late 1990s and launched their own studio in 2007. Two decades on, Onion is trusted to deliver big commissions, including a shopping centre façade for LV The Place Bangkok at Gaysorn Amarin and overhauling the interior of Queen Sirikit National Convention Center. Onion is best known for its work in hospitality – for example, the Sala hotel in Khao Yai (*see page 28*) – so smart hoteliers are advised to seek out the pair at their Sathorn office. Every hotel they design draws upon regional materials, from Ayutthaya's local bricks to the coconuts of Koh Samui.

ARCHITECTURE STUDIO
BODINCHAPA ARCHITECTS
Ayutthaya

Should you move to Thailand with the aim of setting up a café – an apt move, given how seriously the country takes coffee – then you should strongly consider tasking BodinChapa Architects with turning your plans into reality. The founders, Phitchapa Lothong and Bodin Mueanglue, have a strong portfolio of contemporary cafés under their belt, including Kunst Bake'n Cof, Basic Space Coffee, Tewa Ayutthaya and Sonny Coffee & Juice, all based in Ayutthaya. Although they are sensitive to local heritage, their refined yet rustic use of brick, timber and corrugated elements gives their spaces a modern twist. If you need to sort out accommodation too, the firm is also well versed in creating residences: the MYJ House is a lesson in elegance.

ARCHITECTURE STUDIO
SHER MAKER STUDIO
Chiang Mai

Husband and wife team Thongchai Chansamak and Patcharada Inplang (*pictured, on right, with Chansamak*) met in Chiang Mai's craft community before opening a studio together. The duo – both architecture graduates – have a successful background in production-driven business (he, with bamboo bicycles; she, with ceramics and bookbinding) and this passion translates into their portfolio. "We have a mentality of making things ourselves, and not everything we do has to be architectural," says Inplang. Their projects include a workshop in Chiang Mai for Moonler (*see page 197*) and the interior of Aesop's Thonglor shop in Bangkok. "If the project is interesting, we will participate for sure," says Inplang.

PRODUCT DESIGN STUDIO
PDM BRAND
Bangkok

"PDM stands for Product Design Matters – a philosophy rooted in our belief that everyday objects can hold meaning, beauty and cultural value," says Doonyapol Sichan (*pictured*), the brand's co-founder and creative director. As such, the label applies a splash of tasteful craft to common household items in Thai homes, including laundry baskets and pillows. "We want to celebrate Thai culture in a way that feels modern, refined and globally relevant," says Sichan. Furniture and fashion are now part of the range, starting with a recycled-polypropylene housemat inspired by the simple mats seen in temples and rural homes across Southeast Asia. With this, PDM Brand created a durable alternative to carpet – one suited to tropical climates and more visible in contemporary homes.

INTERIOR DESIGN STUDIO
STUDIO FREEHAND
Bangkok

Of the new-wave talent executing some of Thailand's most striking interiors, Studio Freehand is among the leading exponents. Silpakorn University graduates Vitit "Sam" Limpaphatanavanich (*pictured, seated on right*), who worked at hospitality design studio Avroko, and Asi Cherdvivattanasin (*pictured, seated on left*) – whose CV includes Singapore's LTW Designworks – have a process that's dictated by the site, whether old or new. There's no signature aesthetic, though each project has a timeless feel. Seafront restaurant Casa Mare has a breezy, whitewashed quality, yet guest rooms at The StandardX hotel feature sober monochrome. "We don't tie ourselves to just one or two styles," says Sam. "We love to explore possibilities."

Searching for the perfect pieces for your new home?
We highlight two upscale Bangkok-based brands and visit a local
furniture business whose studio and workshop overlooks the
rice fields of Chiang Mai. For contact details, see pages 216—218.

FURNITURE

FURNITURE
CHANINTR CRAFT
Bangkok

Chanintr Sirisant is the first person to call when it is time
to fit out an office, shop, home or upscale resort. Sirisant
has been importing designer furniture to Thailand since
the mid-1990s and Chanintr Craft is a reflection of
his pared-back taste. His showroom in Thonglor is set
across two interconnecting buildings and houses mainly
Scandinavian and Japanese furniture and lighting. It
would be difficult to find a more tasteful selection and
there can be few calmer spaces to contemplate furniture
acquisitions than the courtyard café. "The café is that
spark – the heart of the whole thing," says Sirisant. "It
allows people to feel engaged with the lifestyle that we
are presenting and experience it for themselves."

FURNITURE
ALEXANDER LAMONT
Bangkok

Alexander Lamont (*pictured*) set up in Bangkok at the turn of the century, having lived and studied in Thailand and wishing to draw from the skills and materials of Southeast Asia. His brand releases new collections annually, spanning sculptural tables, parchment-clad cabinets, bronze vessels and warm eggshell and lacquer pendant lighting. "I draw from nature and the workshop itself to compose contemporary work in the great materials of the deco and Edo periods," says Lamont, whose studio is situated above the workshop where every piece is built and processed by hand. For those looking to dress their homes in Thai finery, drop by the extraordinary showroom in Warehouse 30 (*see page 100*).

FURNITURE
MOONLER
Chiang Mai

Moonler's founder, Phuwanat "Banky" Damrongporn (*pictured*), left engineering for a career in furniture-making. His workshop and serene showroom, set among the rice fields of Doi Saket, draw upon the area's rich pool of carpenters and carvers, who turn out chairs, tables, stools and benches using acacia, a local hardwood. "We buy our wood by the log and cure and dry it ourselves," says Banky. The firm launches two collections a year and collaborates with studios from Thailand and abroad. The curvy Pebble Stool 01 and coffee table, made alongside Bangkok's Atelier 2+, is a bestseller. The Phaka Arm Chair by the company's design director, Ratthee Phaisanchotsiri, is a remarkably comfortable perch that's ideal for dining tables.

Finding like-minded contacts, clever collaborators and fun friends makes all the difference when you're setting up a new home or business. Let us introduce you to two social hubs that will help smooth the way. For contact details, see pages 216—218.

BUILD A NETWORK

SOCIAL CLUB

FOREIGN CORRESPONDENTS' CLUB OF THAILAND
Bangkok

Foreign Correspondents' Clubs are storied places for new arrivals to get up to speed on current affairs. This one is on the penthouse floor of the Maneeya Center and the bar and restaurant are where you'll spot the who's who of international media (the balcony view over downtown Bangkok is a go-to backdrop for pieces to camera). Journalists are elected annually to lead the club and use their contact books to deliver a weekly programme of compelling panel discussions, interviews with politicians, film screenings and book launches. Membership is open to all and non-members can attend events for a small fee. As for the dress code: tropical shirts easily outnumber ties and blazers at the bar.

CULTURAL CENTRE
THE COMMONS
Bangkok

At The Commons' maiden site in the Thonglor neighbourhood, co-founders Vicharee and Varatt Vichit-Vadakan offer a more socially orientated hangout space as an alternative to Bangkok's ubiquitous commercial shopping centres. Since opening in 2016 The Commons has quickly blossomed into a launchpad for the small businesses that it hosts. "About a third of the current units have been here since the beginning," says Vicharee. "We curate vendors so there is no overlap in our community." Aside from weekend running clubs, book discussions and meet-ups, it's open with a bar and music until 01.00, seven days a week – and runs its own charitable organisation, Common Compassion.

You've decided where to set up shop, commissioned a talented designer and put a down payment on a chic residence – it's time to meet three expats who've made the move, set up new ventures and now call Thailand home.

SUCCESS STORIES

CHEF
GABRIELA ESPINOSA
Bangkok

Mexico City-born Gabriela Espinosa worked across Asia for 10 years before establishing Delia – a home-from-home Mexican spot that brought her culinary journey full circle. "I knew one day that I would set up my own restaurant," says Espinosa from behind the counter of Delia's bustling kitchen, her gloved hands constructing a seared-pork taco with salsa roja and a crispy mozzarella topping. The result is a deeply Mexican menu with generous sprinklings of Thai influence – the guacamole and chips contains creamy avocados, *pico de gallo* and an infusion of Thai herbs. "Bangkok is a very challenging, exciting city. Being able to slowly build a community here has been a beautifully rewarding experience," Espinosa adds.

ARCHITECT
DAVID SCHAFER
Nonthaburi

RETAILER
ANTOINETTE JACKSON
Chiang Mai

Australian entrepreneur Antoinette Jackson travelled the world before settling in northern Thailand and starting her own business: Superbee. Her sustainable beeswax wraps – an old technique passed down from her grandmother – are made in the hills above Chiang Mai and exported globally. "We came to Chiang Mai for a week and when we saw the moat around the old city we could instantly feel the soul and the depth of the place," she says. A year later, Jackson, a translator and English teacher, packed up her family into a truck and drove from Hua Hin to Chiang Mai. "Moving to Chiang Mai with kids automatically creates a community," says Jackson, who now has her own shop at Chiang Mai International Airport.

As an architecture student at the University of Arizona, David Schafer learned that the desert can be managed by architecture. However, when he moved to Thailand to launch design practice Studiomake with his late wife and partner, Im, he quickly realised that it is almost impossible to curb the tropical climate. Moisture will cause delamination, the sun will bleach colour and the winds will create chaos. Given the challenging conditions, the studio tailors its solutions to every project, as opposed to offering any sort of signature aesthetic or standardised design. "Clients either have a strange project that no one else wants to touch or they have a normal project that they want touched in a strange way," says Schafer. Projects, therefore, are as varied as they are innovative. "Work has ranged from crafting a VIP coin for a Bangkok speakeasy to designing and fabricating a modular structural system for a house project," says Schafer. Other unusual design projects include making grease traps for a mobile espresso cart and collaborating with an artist on kinetic bases for her sculptures.

PART 03

ADDRESS BOOK

Take a tour or plan your next trip with our handy guide to the best
places to eat, stay, shop and see throughout Thailand.

BANGKOK

Thailand's headline act draws droves of travellers who come for the many choices available. Alongside the temples are envelope-pushing restaurants, vibrant street food, dynamic nightlife and a flourishing art landscape. Our take on the capital goes beyond the well-trodden paths.

STAY

NA TANAO 1969
Old Town
Packed into a slender townhouse that stands just 3.5 metres wide, this Bangkok-based "hometel" is steeped in rich family history, with ancestral relics scattered throughout.
natanao1969.com

CAPELLA BANGKOK
Sathorn
The unobstructed view of the Chao Phraya river affords Capella Bangkok one of the most coveted locations in the city. Each guest pad features a balcony that looks onto the scene in front.
capellahotels.com

PUBLIC HOUSE
Soi Sawatdi
A colourful wall mural by Spanish-Mexican artist Rafael Uriegas greets arrivals to Public House and immediately sets the tone for this lively independent hotel just north of Sukhumvit Road.
publichouse-hotels.com

MANDARIN ORIENTAL
Charoen Krung
The Mandarin Oriental, Thailand's oldest international hotel, dates back nearly 150 years. Guests new and old come here to experience the country's famed hospitality.
mandarinoriental.com

THE SUKHOTHAI
Sathorn
An old-world bubble of calm among the downtown chaos. Its stall is set out across hushed pavilions, well-kept gardens, a courtyard and lotus ponds.
bangkok.sukhothai.com

AMAN NAI LERT BANGKOK
Pathum Wan
Surrounded by the verdant greenery of the capital's 2.8-hectare Nai Lert Park, this select bolthole prioritises privacy and luxury, and offers 52 plush suites, a state-of-the-art spa and a wellness centre.
aman.com

GRAND HYATT ERAWAN BANGKOK
Pathum Wan
There are few spots better tailored for Bangkok's business community. The hotel sits on the doorstep of several major retail destinations.
hyatt.com

ROSEWOOD
Pathum Wan
This outpost has deployed sophisticated fit-outs comprising plush furnishings, rattan accents and marble bathrooms, with glass walls allowing for floods of natural light.
rosewoodhotels.com

THE SIAM
Dusit
Of all the five-star hotels that line Bangkok's Chao Phraya river, The Siam is one of the few owned and operated by a Thai family.
thesiamhotel.com

FOOD & DRINK

BO.LAN
Thonglor
Chefs Duangporn "Bo" Songvisava and Dylan Jones showcase the breadth of the country's traditional recipes, serving time-honoured dishes such as sugarcane-steamed chicken.
bolan.co.th

BAAN TROK TUA NGORK
Yaowarat
What was a time-worn, underutilised family home is now a spirited hangout in Chinatown, replete with a class of boundary-pushing restaurants and bars.
baantrok.com

BA HAO TIAN MI
Yaowarat
This dessert parlour reimagines Thai-Chinese sweet treats for a modern palate. You can enjoy gojiberry pudding and a bowl of black sesame soup with *taro mochi*.
8 Phadung Dao Rd

KAIZEN COFFEE
Ekkamai
Light-filled and airy, Arnun Wattanaporn's Ekkamai café is beloved for its first-rate offerings, ranging from long blacks to cold-brews and creative sourdough toppings to innovative pastas.
kaizencoffee.com

CURVY DINING
Krungthep Kreeta
The light, bright, white flower-shaped pavilion that is Curvy Dining makes no apologies for its ultra-graphic presence in southeast Bangkok.
8 Soi Srinakarin-Romklao 19

FREAKING OUT THE NEIGHBOURHOOD
Thonglor
Kitted out with vintage JBL speakers and a McIntosh amp, this bar treats each night's music like a festival line-up, presenting a mix of live complementary acts ahead of the night's featured album.
freakingout.co

SMALLS
Sathorn
A sultry, eccentric space, Smalls is the place to head for an evening of jazz. It hosts a rich mix of Thai talent and internationally renowned musicians.
186/3—4 Suan Phlu 1 Soi

YELLOW LANE
Ari
An Aussie-flavoured, all-day restaurant housed in one of Ari's typical mid-century modernist houses, Yellow Lane is a popular gathering spot in this leafy residential neighbourhood.
2, 92 Soi Phahon Yothin 5

BAAN DUSIT THANI
Sala Daeng
Set in a heritage house, Baan Dusit Thani is home to popular Thai and Vietnamese restaurants, Benjarong and Thien Duong, as well as the quiet Dusit Gourmet café and convivial South American restaurant Nómada.
baandusitthani.com

THE NORM
Silom
The Norm's outdoor terrace looks out over downtown Bangkok. On big nights, the decks will be spinning in two venues at once: The Main Hall and The Terrace, The Norm's outdoor spritz bar.
thenormbangkok.com

KAD KOKOA
Sathorn
As the gold standard of Thai chocolate – preferred by pastry chefs at many of Thailand's five-star hotels – Kad Kokoa's distinctive square chocolate bars are named according to the origin of the beans.
kadkokoa.com

TEP BAR
Yaowarat
To enter this restored shophouse is to be immersed in a compelling fusion of traditional cuisine and modern hospitality. Home to live house bands, performances using traditional Thai instruments fill the air with an inviting beat.
69, 81 Soi Nana, Charoen Krung Rd

POTONG
Yaowarat
Originally an apothecary, the building where Potong is located retains its restorative charm with a rooftop garden where guests can choose from a Thai-Chinese menu while they enjoy the sunset.
restaurantpotong.com

CHARMKRUNG
Talat Noi
On the sixth floor of an unassuming building, this Thai tapas bar is a 60-cover establishment for anyone looking to escape the city bustle and settle in for a culinary treat.
6th floor, 839 Charoen Krung Rd

SUNDRY
Lumpini
Nestled in an orange building, the warm radiance of this backlit bar is inspired by sunlight. The flattering glow ensures that it is always golden hour when you're sipping a cocktail.
1018 8 Rama IV Rd

KARO
Pridi
Karo has been the hottest spot for a casual hangout since its opening, with tables that spill out under shaded awnings – the best seats in the house on cooler mornings.
52 Soi Pridi Banomyong 26

GAGGAN
Sukhumvit 31
The centerpiece is a 14-seat chef's counter, where a 22-course tasting menu unfolds below a disco ball and colourful lights, accompanied by an upbeat playlist.
gaggan.com

DELIA
Yaowarat
The brainchild of Mexico City-born Gabriela Espinosa, Delia's Mexican menu has plenty of Thai influence – try the guacamole, which contains a profusion of herbs.
baandelia.com

ALONE TOGETHER
Soi Sawatdi
Live music takes centre stage at Alone Together, an intimate jazz bar. Low seating and attentive table service invite guests to enjoy the experience with a cocktail.
sugarraygroup.com/alonetogether

CITIZEN TEA CANTEEN
Talat Noi
A cross between a traditional Chinese tea house and a colourful eclectic showroom. You'll find an array of local crafts and creations alongside a wide variety of blends.
764 Soi Wanit 2

KAENKRUNG
Bangkok Noi
Dishes from Isan, local produce and a playlist featuring jazz and funky *molam* all come together at this casual spot in west Bangkok.
521/11 Arun Marin Rd

ROOTS
Thonglor
As one of Thailand's most respected speciality roasters, Roots' approach is simple: great coffee brewed with beans carefully chosen to best fit your personal tastes.
17 Thonglor

THIPSAMAI
Old Town
Hailed as the restaurant that pioneered pad thai in 1939, the simple menu includes spring rolls and refreshing drinks, though we recommend the dish that started it all: the Superb Pad Thai.
thipsamai.com

APPIA
Soi Sawatdi
Appia offers a culinary journey into Rome's Testaccio neighbourhood. The pasta is made fresh daily and served in a warmly lit interior where the walls are lined with wine bottles.
20/4 Sukhumvit 31, Klongton Nua Watthana

THE ADDRESS BOOK | BANGKOK

SHOP

JBB
Chidlom
Jirawat "Bote" Benchakarn's menswear label offers comfortable linen tailoring and breathable Oxford button-downs cut to accentuate a strong silhouette. There are informal pieces too, such as safari jackets.
jbbmenswear.com

VVON SUGUNNASIL
Sathorn
Bangkok's fashionable crowd head to Vvon Sugunnasil for bespoke suits, formal gowns and other outfits for special occasions.
vvonsugunnasil.com

CHANINTR CRAFT
Thonglor
Chanintr Sirisant is the first person to call upon when it is time to fit out an office, style a shop, furnish a home or decorate an upscale resort.
chanintr.com

SIAM PARAGON
Siam
Located in central Bangkok and served by Siam BTS station, the busiest on the city's Skytrain elevated rail network, Siam Paragon is a hub for luxury shopping.
siamparagon.com

CONTAINER
Siam
Kanit Tantiwong's accessories label is known for its totes, wallets and folios, all of which use high-quality leather and have a stripped-back style.
containerbag.net

EMQUARTIER
Phrom Phong
Alongside heavyweight brands and homegrown labels, this shopping centre also houses seven cinema screens, six storeys of dining terraces and a manmade waterfall.
emquartier.co.th

ZUDRANGMA RECORDS
Thonglor
Zudrangma Records stocks the best in Thai music – and whether it's *molam* (traditional storytelling) or *luk thung* folk, the broad collection is entirely handpicked by the owner.
zudrangmarecords.com

PANA OBJECTS
Lumpini
Pana Objects is focused on one material: wood. Most of the product range consists of measured, well-executed examples of homewares that are often overlooked.
pana-objects.com

CHATUCHAK WEEKEND MARKET
Chatuchak
With more than 15,000 stalls, Chatuchak Weekend Market is an energising, sun-baked maze of clothing, apothecary goods, Thai crafts, ceramics, furniture, street food, plants and more.
587/10 Kamphaeng Phet 2 Rd

EASTERN GLASS
Bang Khae
Housed within a renovated factory on the outskirts of Bangkok, Eastern Glass is the oldest working glass manufacturer in the country.
480 Phet Kasem Rd

WAREHOUSE 30
Charoen Krung
A 20-minute walk from Chinatown, Warehouse 30 is an enclave of selected retail and design units that unfold via a long corridor threading each consecutive plot together.
warehouse30.com

THE DECORUM
Ari
Catering to all aspects of a modern gent's wardrobe, stock includes made-to-measure suits hand-sewn in South Korea, Echizenya trousers and shoes from Baudoin & Lange.
thedecorumbkk.com

CENTRAL WORLD
Pathum Wan
Amid the glitz and glass, traffic and towers of Pathum Wan, Central World houses an attractive list of destinations, including fashion labels, beauty brands, watch houses and homeware shops.
central.co.th

ALEXANDER LAMONT
Charoen Krung
Alexander Lamont's annual collections feature parchment-clad cabinets, bronze vessels, warm eggshell and lacquer pendant lighting, and sculptural tables covered with raw surfaces.
alexanderlamont.com

THE COMMONS
Thonglor
At The Commons' maiden site in the Thonglor neighbourhood, founder Vicharee Vichit-Vadakan offers a more socially orientated hangout space as an alternative to the numerous commercial shopping centres nearby.
thecommonsbkk.com

ARCHIVES DESIGN
Ratchathewi
Archives Design collaborates with an array of artists to create pieces that redefine the boundaries of leather craftsmanship. Timeless pieces include jewellery boxes and Christmas ornaments.
archives-design.com

PAÑPURI
Chidlom
An ode to Thailand's unique wellness culture, Pañpuri's range of hand creams, face cleansers and perfume oils combines organic ingredients with Thai plants including jasmine, lemongrass and sandalwood.
panpuri.com

PRONTO ORIGINAL
Siam
Founder Chnanon Sachdev noticed the quality of Japanese denim and saw a gap in the market. Offshoots of this multi-label shop can now be found across the city.
prontooriginal.com

ASAVA
Sukhumvit 45
Polpat "Moo" Asavaprapha is one of Thailand's leading fashion figures – and once a new Asava collection drops, shoppers arrive in droves to secure his latest designs.
asavagroup.com

ONION
Ekkamai
This clothing retailer stocks men's- and womenswear, selling garments from its own line as well as other specially selected items from around the globe.
onionbkk.com

PDM BRAND
Suan Luang
PDM Brand applies a splash of tasteful craft and eye-catching colour to household items in Thai homes, including laundry baskets, tissue boxes and cushion covers.
pdmbrand.com

PATCHARAVIPA
Pathum Wan
Patcharavipa has gained a cult following for its handcrafted jewellery collections that draw upon rare, precious and unconventional materials, including coconut shells.
patcharavipa.com

CHABATREE
Lat Phrao
Home and kitchenware brand Chabatree is committed to using exclusively Thai wood at its workshop in northern Thailand to create its fetching made-in-Thailand kitchen utensils.
chabatree.com

DO

FOREIGN CORRESPONDENTS' CLUB OF THAILAND
Pathum Wan
Anchoring the penthouse floor of the Maneeya Center, this lively spot is ideal for new arrivals interested in getting up to speed on current affairs. Membership is open to all.
fccthai.com

BANGKOK KUNSTHALLE
Yaowarat
Bangkok's emergence as a leading Southeast Asian contemporary-art hub owes much to the Bangkok Kunsthalle. A private art institution, the venue is both a contemporary gallery and an architectural conservation project.
khaoyaiart.com

OPEN HOUSE
Phloen Chit
Open House unfolds to reveal pillars loaded with plastic-wrapped rare editions of cult magazines, two levels of wall-to-wall shelving and a space dedicated to pop-up books and art installations. There's a fine array of dining options too.
centralembassy.com

NUMTHONG ART SPACE
Ari
This gallery is a magnet for contemporary art lovers, exhibiting local and internationally renowned artists with a strong emphasis on emerging talent.
numthongartspace.com

MUSEUM OF CONTEMPORARY ART
Chatuchak
Presenting art from talent across the country in a light-filled setting, MOCA showcases Thai greats such as surrealist artist Prateep Kochabua and stalwarts of the art scene including Thawan Duchanee.
mocabangkok.com

EMBASSY DIPLOMAT SCREENS
Phloen Chit
This swanky cinema on the top floor of Central Embassy has premium draws, such as daybeds, soft blankets, plumped pillows, mini bars and even butler service.
embassycineplex.com

RAJADAMNERN STADIUM
Old Town
Rajadamnern Stadium is Thailand's oldest Muay Thai arena and provides an authentic experience of watching the sport. Matches are loud and wild, with thousands of combat fans packing the auditorium.
rajadamnern.com

THE QUEEN SIRIKIT MUSEUM OF TEXTILES
Old Town
During her extensive royal tenure, Queen Sirikit was celebrated as a fashion icon. Key pieces can be admired from within this venue's various galleries.
qsmtthailand.org

JIM THOMPSON ART CENTER
Siam
Bangkok's cultural scene is booming and the capital's art aficionados flock to this purpose-built centre for its programme of exhibitions that feature marginalised voices and regional works.
jimthompsonartcenter.org

RQ SPORT
Sukhumvit
Pools, rooftop tennis courts and an indoor rock-climbing set-up can be found in this mixed-use fitness hub.
rqclub.com

DIB BANGKOK
Sukhumvit
A venue housing contemporary works in a one-time steel warehouse that features raw concrete pillars and an outdoor sculpture garden.
dibbangkok.org

BANGKOK

THE ADDRESS BOOK

NORTH

Thailand's northern reaches are reputed for their dramatic scenery of waterfalls, jungles and mountains with a cinematic feel. Our suggestions are largely based in Chiang Rai (go for the tea plantations and the art scene) and Chiang Mai (Lan Na cuisine, with its earthy dishes, is one of life's great pleasures).

STAY

TATVANI
Chiang Rai
As a one-key, 11.7-hectare private estate spread across six villas with accommodation for a total of 18 guests, Tatvani is one of the most luxurious – and peaceful – places to stay in Thailand.
tatvani.com

TAMARIND VILLAGE
Chiang Mai
Guests enter Tamarind Village – named after the 200-year-old tree in the courtyard – via a bamboo-lined driveway. The natural canopy creates a sense of calm and peace that permeates the rest of the property.
tamarindvillage.com

137 PILLARS
Chiang Mai
At the centre of this tranquil 30-key, all-suite property is the historic teak HQ of a British trade company supported on 137 pillars, which now houses the hotel's bar, restaurant, library, shop and gym.
137pillarshotels.com

RAYA HERITAGE
Chiang Mai
Every detail of Raya Heritage, from the architecture and furniture to textiles and incidental objects, has an underlying raison d'être: to connect with the local Lan Na culture.
rayaheritage.com

RACHAMANKHA
Chiang Mai
Designed to reflect traditional Lan Na architecture, interlinked courtyards and collonaded pavilions provide a graceful setting for hotelier Rooj Changtrakul's collection of antiques.
rachamankha.com

FOOD & DRINK

SAWANBONDIN TEA HOUSE & EXPERIENCE
Chiang Rai
On the outskirts of Chiang Rai city, Sawanbondin – which translates as "heaven on Earth" – is a tea house devoted to quiet appreciation of its brews.
171/12 Village 1

SANGKAEW
Chiang Rai
Enjoy Burmese tea – picked on a family plantation in Myanmar – and a tray of *kengtung* and northern Thai specialities, while dipping your toes in the adjacent stream.
1208 Mae Kon

BLACKITCH ARTISAN KITCHEN
Chiang Mai
In this 18-seat restaurant on the second floor of a narrow city-centre shophouse, a 10-course menu is constantly adapted according to the seasons. We recommend one dish in particular: jungle curry (*kaeng paa*).
blackitch.com

KANVELA
Chiang Mai
Kanvela's award-winning tree-to-bar chocolate business is founded on ethical and fair-trade farming practices, spanning basic bars to intricately decorated bonbons and even teas made from cacao husks.
kanvelachocolate.com

KAMSLA
Chiang Mai
Nassapong Chansukhon set up his one-table restaurant in his garden in Saraphi. His lunch-only sittings must be booked in advance and cater for intimate parties of two to six.
23/3 Village 4 Soi Wat Chang Kheng

LOCUS NATIVE FOOD LAB
Chiang Rai
Chef Kong has a mission to celebrate northern Thai cuisine and does so at his 12-seat chef's table restaurant in a corner of the Tatvani hotel.
locusnativefoodlab.com

KHAGEE
Chiang Mai
Owned and run by Thai-Japanese couple Thames and Miki, everything served at Khagee is homemade. We recommend the mini cylinders of carrot cake with cream-cheese icing.
29/30 Chiang Mai-Lamphun 1 Soi

THE HOUSE BY GINGER
Chiang Mai
The contentment-inducing ambience at The House by Ginger is the creation of Danish designer Hans Bøgetoft Christensen and the equally artful menu is packed with Thai favourites.
thehousebygingercm.com

MA LONG DER
Chiang Rai
The cuisine at this riverside spot doesn't stray far from authentic Lan Na fare. The creativity that goes into the dishes means that they are as wonderful to look at as they are to eat.
551 Village 1 Phahonyothin Rd

ANOTHER SMITH
Tak
Bamboo is used to spectacular effect in this restaurant, making for a remarkable setting in which to enjoy the Thai-Chinese cuisine. Try the soft-shell crab fried with garlic.
666 Village 2, Asia Highway, Tha Sai Luat

SHOP

LONG GOY
Chiang Mai
Set among rice fields, the bright blue, two-storey studio makes a striking statement, as does the clothing, which lies somewhere between bespoke high fashion and street art.
120 San Klang

DOY DIN DANG POTTERY
Chiang Rai
Doy Din Dang's property is home to half a dozen small buildings, including a gallery, shop and café, all of which are surrounded, inlaid or filled with artist Somluk Pantiboon's work.
Nang Lae

WIT'S COLLECTION
Chiang Mai
Owner Wisut Limaree has been importing handmade creations from across Asia since the 1980s, and his expertise plays out in a space that feels as much like a gallery as a shop, with treasures in many hues, materials and sizes.
198 Village 4, T.Baan Waen

AKALIKO
Chiang Mai
Akaliko is a champion of minimal contemporary design, stocking fine examples of the owners' work, including bowls, coffee cups, candle holders and vases made from hand-turned teak.
akalikodesignshop.com

VILA CINI
Chiang Mai
As a renowned purveyor of luxury Thai silk products, Vila Cini offers a stunning selection of high-end handmade items in saturated colourways, including cushion covers, scarves, bags, clothing and chic slippers.
vilacini.com

KALM VILLAGE
Chiang Mai
With no fewer than three lifestyle stores, Kalm Village stocks an array of beautiful handmade clothing, homewares and jewellery, all of which are designed in-house and produced in collaboration with local artisans.
kalmvillage.com

EARTH & FIRE CERAMICS
Lampang
Earth & Fire Ceramics makes the kind of crockery that you come across in tasteful uptown restaurants. The premises house a workshop, factory and studio, an art gallery, a relaxing café and a shop.
371 Lampang Luang

PALIT
Chiang Mai
Palit started out with beautifully made contemporary macramé and crochet bags that still feature in its collections but it's the clothing made from natural fibres that epitomise the brand today.
palitpalit.myshopify.com

SOP MOEI ARTS
Chiang Mai
Having observed the exceptional weaving skills of the Pwo Karen tribes, founder Kent Gregory began an artistic collaboration concentrating on richly coloured textiles that are still at the heart of Sop Moei Arts' offerings today.
sopmoeiarts.com

DO

DHARMA PARK AND INSON WONGSAM ART GALLERY
Lamphun
Pioneering Thai artist Inson Wongsam lived and worked in Paris before returning to his hometown of Lamphun, where a private museum, sculpture garden and café are located alongside his home and studio.
inson-wongsam.com

BAAN DAM MUSEUM
Chiang Rai
Praised for his provocative style that was heavily influenced by spiritual and mystic themes, artist Thawan Duchanee's influence is evident at the Baan Dam Museum.
333 Nang Lae

CHIANG RAI CONTEMPORARY ART MUSEUM
Chiang Rai
Within this glass-and-steel structure, generous double-height spaces host a programme of exhibitions displaying the work of contemporary Thai artists. The café offers fine views over the surrounding rice fields.
Tambon Rim Kok

THE BOOKSMITH
Chiang Mai
The Booksmith occupies the ground floor of a shophouse and former art gallery, where visitors can browse art, design and lifestyle books that can't be found elsewhere.
thebooksmith.co.th

ARAKSA TEA GARDEN
Chiang Mai
Araksa Tea Garden invites its guests to pick tea and have tastings in the shop. The award-winning organic teas are served in the Thai capital's smartest hotels and exported around the world.
araksatea.com

MAIIAM
Chiang Mai
This future-facing contemporary art destination displays the private collection of Thai and Asian art accumulated by Parisian gallerist Jean Michel Beurdeley, his late wife Patsri Bunnag, and their son, Eric Bunnag Booth.
maiiam.com

NORTH

THE ADDRESS BOOK

NORTHEAST

Even though it covers a third of the country, the northeast, also called Isan, remains fairly underexplored and underrated. A mix of influences from neighbouring countries trickles into the fabric of the region. Khon Kaen is the perfect base from which to explore the area.

STAY

SALA
Khao Yai
Guests of this boutique chain get to stay in standalone villas with individual gardens, private swimming pools and uninterrupted views of the surrounding hillsides.
salahospitality.com

AD LIB
Khon Kaen
The crowning glory of the 28-storey Khon Kaen Innovation Center building, this unabashedly sleek modern hotel offers a rooftop pool, live music venue and two restaurants.
adlibhotels.co

SUPANNIGA HOME
Khon Kaen
With its sprawling grounds and sleek cottages, this secluded hotel is among the best places to stay in Khon Kaen. Three villas vie for attention, with a restaurant serving recipes by the owner's grandmother.
130/9 Photisan Rd

FOOD & DRINK

BOOUY BAR
Khon Kaen
This neon bar is intensified by an electric atmosphere that comes courtesy of the spirited conversations, the buzz of live music and the cheers directed towards the on-screen sports.
348 18—19 Thanon Ruen Rom 1

SEE NA NUAN CAFÉ
Khon Kaen
Acknowledged by locals and critics alike as one of the northeastern town's must-visit places, See Na Nuan Café is a well-practised purveyor of some of Khon Kaen's most deeply flavoured food.
164/160 Village 14, Tawan Mai Rd

GRANMONTE ESTATE
Khao Yai
Khao Yai is known for its sprawling national park but it has cultivated another draw: wine. At the heart of this shift is Granmonte Estate and its 100 per cent Khao Yai-grown wines.
granmonte.com

MOK
Ubon Ratchathani
Named after the traditional Thai technique of steaming food, Mok is a converted two-storey home that serves hearty Thai dishes.
115 Phrommarat Rd

RUSTY-SOCIAL CLUB
Khon Kaen
Crowds come to hear the most thrilling new local acts performing original music and covers of smash-hit singalongs on the sizeable stage. Open from 18.00 until 01.00.
150/152 Sri Chant Rd

SAMUAY & SONS
Udon Thani
Focused on regional Isan cuisine, Samuay & Sons' menu features healthy home-style cooking that makes use of seasonal and local produce wherever possible.
208/9 Mueang District Rd

KAEN
Khon Kaen
In an unassuming backstreet, Kaen is quietly making some of the most exciting Thai and Isan cuisine outside of Bangkok, using fresh, locally sourced ingredients.
140/64 Soi Adulyaram 3 Nai Mueang

SHOP

DON MOO DIN
Sakon Nakhon
Don Moo Din – a pottery company owned by Walriya Pengsawang – sells beautiful, natural earthenware that deserves pride of place in anyone's special-occasion cabinet.
12 Village 5, Ngiew Don

BAN NAKHA SILK MARKET
Udon Thani
Sheltered from the chaos of the Udon Thani-Nong Khai highway, Ban Nakha Silk Market is a long and lively covered street where purveyors of Isan's biggest trade gather to display and sell their handmade products.
Mueang Udon Thani

DO

MOLAM BUS
Nakhon Ratchasima
When not attending the Wonderfruit festival, the Molam Bus is a mobile exhibition dedicated to the sounds and culture of Isan, Thailand's northeastern region.
jimthompsonfarm.com

THAILAND CREATIVE & DESIGN CENTER
Khon Kaen
A government-funded initiative with a mission to support the country's creative talent. There are standalone buildings in Bangkok, Chiang Mai, Khon Kaen and Songkhla.
tcdc.or.th

KHAO YAI ART FOREST
Khao Yai
At Khao Yai Art Forest, site-specific works by contemporary names and installations from the permanent collection are positioned across the 85-hectare site. Many of them are substantial and spectacular.
khaoyaiart.com

EAST

The east is ideal for those after a beach escape without the crowds of Phuket or Koh Samui. Being in easy reach of Bangkok also means city activity is never too far away. Excellent seafood and an abundance of tropical fruit (it is Thailand's largest fruit-producing region) add to the allure.

STAY

KOH MUNNORK
Koh Man Nok
On this private island, electricity is shut off for several hours each morning. Guests are encouraged to practice mindfulness and to make the most of the sunlight.
munnorkprivateisland.com

PARADEE
Koh Samet
Getting its name from the Sanskrit word for paradise, Paradee's sunny yellow interiors and comforting nooks are all beautifully finished with hardwood trims.
paradeethesixthheaven.com

ANDAZ HOTEL
Pattaya
The 204-key shoreline retreat is set across six hectares and the 18 varieties of rooms range from stunning 50 sq m dwellings with garden views to a three-bedroom beachfront heritage house.
hyatt.com

THE STANDARD
Pattaya
This brand's third hotel in Thailand is located on Jomtien Beach. The 161-key coastal property has a branded beach club called Esmé, where seafood-inspired Mexican cuisine is overseen by Gaby Espinosa, chef-owner of Bangkok's highly regarded Delia.
standardhotels.com

THE DEWA KOH CHANG
Koh Chang
Embracing the "tropical rustic" aesthetic, this hotel has exposed concrete walls and double-height timber ceilings topped by thatched or shingled roofs.
thedewakohchang.com

MASON
Pattaya
Offering ultra-modern villas, Mason is on the coast south of Jomtien beach, in a cultural enclave that is home to a community of contemporary artisans.
masonpattaya.com

THE RETREAT
Koh Chang
Local carpenters reused 100-year-old teak reclaimed from abandoned houses in northern Thailand to build this Japanese-inspired, 38-key hotel.
theretreatkohchang.com

FOOD & DRINK

DRIFT BAR
Rayong
A reliably fun crowd gathers for sundowners at this relaxed beach bar run by three siblings.
Ao Khai Beach

EASTERLY
Chanthaburi
By day, grab a coffee and sit on the porch. At night, espresso martinis go well with the entertainment, including DJs and guest mixologists who spice up the menu from visit to visit.
182 Sukhaphiban Rd

KHAO KWAN
Koh Chang
This conceptual, contemporary Thai kitchen serves small and colourful plates that erupt with flavour, often decorated with delicate bouquets of small flowers.
51/5, Village 4

THE GARDENER
Chanthaburi
This elegant café is tucked in among a string of shops near the Chanthaburi river. As well as hot drinks, it serves sweet treats and frozen smoothies, emphasising the natural elements from which it earns its name.
Maharaj Rd

CAP
Chanthaburi
Quaintly acronymic, Cap stands for "Café and People", a name inspired by the drive to provide the area with a wholesome, modern hangout spot where people can linger with a coffee.
161/2 Sukhaphiban Rd

ROCKET ICE CREAM
Chanthaburi
With more than 50 years of gelaterie experience, Rocket Ice Cream is a shiny street-side spot. Durian and Thai iced tea are among the plethora of fun and unique flavours.
255—7 Sukhaphiban Rd

HARUDOT
Chon Buri
Designed by IDIN Architects, this café houses large, mature trees, including a 100-year-old baobab, which is distinctive for it's bottle-shaped trunk. The offering includes a "speed bar" with an espresso machine and a "slow bar" for handmade brews.
nanacoffeeroasters.com

DO

WONDERFRUIT FESTIVAL
Chon Buri
Crowds come here in their droves for live music, art installations, wellness activities and talks. The annual festival also places emphasis on eco-conscious living.
wonderfruit.co

CENTRAL

King Rama VI turbocharged Hua Hin's reputation when he set up a summer palace there in 1924. Known as the Hamptons of Thailand, the resort is a popular getaway for Bangkok families. Elsewhere, the Khao Sam Roi Yot National Park and Ayutthaya Historical Park provide a sense of adventure.

STAY

CHIVA-SOM
Hua Hin
From the get-go, this resort has been a headline draw for affluent travellers looking to reset in style, with a rich programme of fitness classes, treatments and organic fare.
chivasom.com

THE STANDARD
Hua Hin
From the towering rain trees at the entrance to the handsome mid-century-style decor, much of which comes in striking yellow hues, this hotel is a tasteful touch of paradise in this seaside town.
standardhotels.com

Z9 RESORT
Kanchanaburi
A nature lover's paradise, Z9 Resort has a private pontoon for swimming and kayaking, while the waterfalls of Sai Yok and Erawan national parks are nearby.
z9resorts.com

BAAN POMPHET
Ayutthaya
Designed by Bangkok studio Onion, this eight-room waterfront hotel and restaurant is built much like a fortress, recognisable for its distinctive orange-hued brick.
baanpomphet.com

THE BARAI
Hua Hin
Sitting on almost 1.8 hectares of beachfront, the guest rooms boast private plunge pools, personalised butler service and pristine views of the Gulf of Thailand.
thebarai.com

FOOD & DRINK

THE ARTISANS
Ayutthaya
This reservation-only restaurant employs women from the local community as a means of preserving traditional cooking techniques. It is ideal for fans of authentic cuisine and is served with a side of world-class Thai architecture.
theartisansayutthaya.com

PRAÇA
Hua Hin
A playful interpretation of Thai street food, this breezy hangout is part of The Standard and resides in a heritage house with front-row views of the beach.
pracahuahin.com

BAAN TA NID
Pathum Thani
In a riverside setting, guests dine on plates of simple and flavoursome local cuisine, with everything from fried shrimp to grilled catfish on offer, all of it freshly caught earlier in the day.
40 Krachaeng

SUAN THIP
Nonthaburi
Perched on the banks of the Chao Phraya river, Suan Thip has several dining areas among the landscaped gardens, while tables set on the charmingly decorated terrace overlook the river.
17/9 Sukkhaprachasan 2

RORSORI27
Nonthaburi
Guests are served in a family or supper-club style here, on a long, narrow table. Patrons can converse with one another and enjoy their meal as wine is poured by the light of the setting sun.
rorsori27.com

SHOP

KORAKOT AROMDEE
Phetchaburi
This brand manufactures large-scale bamboo sculptures and decorative items for venues worldwide. The work is rooted in Korakot Aromdee's generational knowledge of 12th-century knot-tying techniques and personal interest in craftsmanship.
korakotaromdee.com

CENTRAL AYUTTHAYA
Ayutthaya
Part of the Central Group, this extensive shopping centre is known for its distinctive architecture by Bangkok-based Onion. The firm expresses traditional Ayutthaya style through a contemporary filter.
centralpattana.co.th

DO

THAI FILM ARCHIVE
Nakhon Pathom
The Thai Film Archive preserves and restores a rich library of newsreels, documentaries, feature films and clips while organising a programme of film-related events for visitors.
fapot.or.th

MARUEKHATHAIYAWAN PALACE
Cha-am
Built for King Rama VI, the palace comprises 18 teak buildings connected by balconies, verandas and staircases. The cultural heritage site is open to the public year round.
Phet Kasem Rd

PHUKET

Phuket is the country's largest island and has long been a go-to for the classic sand-and-sea experience. It has become a hub for five-star accommodation: Rosewood and Amanpuri are just some of our beds of choice and it would be remiss to not see the rows of pastel-coloured Sino-Portuguese shophouses.

STAY

TRISARA
Choeng Thale
The hillside stay takes inspiration from southern Thai *mondop* architecture, as seen in the tiered terracotta-tile roofs arranged in layered peaks. Bleached-teak sundecks invite lazy hours in the heat.
trisara.com

THE NAKA PHUKET
Kamala
Designed by Duangrit Bunnag Architect in 2012, the geometric glass-and-concrete villas overhang the sloping mountainside, creating the illusion of floating rooms.
thenakaphuket.com

ROSEWOOD
Patong
Of Thailand's many island hotels, Rosewood Phuket is a standout. Days here are spent dozing on sundecks, being pampered at the Asaya spa and strolling on the shoreline of Emerald Bay.
rosewoodhotels.com

AMANPURI
Choeng Thale
Settled within coconut palms and climbing bougainvillaea, Amanpuri is a paean to the Buddhist architecture of ancient Ayutthaya, with temple-like structures that encourage outdoor living.
aman.com

FOOD & DRINK

SAMUT
Old Town
With a name that means "ocean" in Thai, Samut puts the riches of the sea at the heart of a meticulously crafted, multi-course tasting menu.
samutphuket.com

BLUE ELEPHANT
Old Town
This restaurant's main attraction is the Peranakan menu, a fusion of Thai and Hokkien-Chinese culinary traditions and flavours inspired by Phuketian heritage.
blueelephant.com

TORRY'S
Old Town
Torry's pulls in visitors with premium Phuketian flavours. The traditional Bi-Co-Moi dessert can be found reinvented and other difficult-to-resist flavours include red bean, *bee pang* and yuzu.
torrys.com

ONE CHUN
Old Town
Radiating comfort with its display of personal photos and hearty aromas, the dining room at One Chun is akin to that of a family home.
48/1 Thep Krasattri Rd

THE DISTILLERY PHUKET
Chalong
Visitors are shown behind the scenes on hourly tours before being invited to dine at the bamboo-clad, farm-led bistro and then shake up their own cocktails.
thedistilleryphuket.com

TU KAB KHAO
Old Town
Tu Kab Khao's menu is an ode to traditional southern Thai cuisine, combining a heady mix of aromatic spices, succulent meat and vibrant colours.
8 Phangnga Rd

RESTAURANT ROYD
Old Town
The team at Royd, led by chef Mond, prepares dishes that celebrate the flavours and traditions of southern Thai cuisine, offering a hearty fine-dining experience.
restaurantroyd.com

SHOP

PAINT PALETTE
Old Town
You'll find light, breezy clothing and accessories that are perfect for the heat, such as linen shirts with shell detailing, woven rattan bags, seagrass hats and more.
136 Thalang Rd

ES PHUKET
Old Town
Buried in the crowded streets of Talat Nuea, ES Phuket is a melting pot of contemporary fashion trends and traditional Thai designs.
8 Ratsada Rd

NAKAMOL
Old Town
The designs at Nakamol benefit from an understanding of emerging trends, as well as the refined quality inherent to Thai craftsmanship.
nakamol.com

DO

PHUKET ART VILLAGE
Rawai
Visitors can observe artists working in their studios, partake in various fairs and festivals and take home a one-of-a-kind piece of their own.
2 Soi Naya

PHUKET THAIHUA MUSEUM
Old Town
This museum explores the rich history of the first Chinese immigrants who settled on the island of Phuket during the 19th and early 20th centuries.
phuketthaihuamuseum.com

SOUTH

The south's marquee attraction, Koh Samui, is no longer thought of as an obscure, untouched destination – but there's still beauty in its mountains and palm-fringed beaches. Bliss can also be found on other islands, such as Koh Phangan, which has many quiet enclaves, despite its reputation for parties.

STAY

HAADTIEN BEACH RESORT
Koh Tao
This restorative retreat offers the best of barefoot luxury. Guests can opt to stay nestled within the lush landscape of a coconut plantation or on the shore of Shark Bay.
haadtien.com

RAYAVADEE RESORT
Krabi
Rayavadee Resort is a class apart, with coconut groves swaying in the breeze and a sweet coastal scent drifting along the pathways that lead to the hotel's two-storey pavilions.
rayavadee.com

THANYAMUNDRA
Khao Sok
Decked out with six rooms and a full-length Olympic swimming pool, the site is perched on the threshold between the rainforest edge and the rolling hills of the Khao Sok national park.
thanyamundra.com

DEVASOM KHAO LAK
Khao Lak
At Devasom even the most indecisive traveller will want for nothing, whether you're one for a scenic horizon-edge pool, a Michelin meal, spa treatments or private cooking classes.
devasom.com

KAMALAYA
Koh Samui
Dreamt up by a former monk and a doctor of traditional Chinese medicine, this holistic wellness retreat is a meeting point of eastern traditions and western practices.
kamalaya.com

BABA ECOLODGE
Koh Phra Thong
On the rugged, barely touched island of Koh Phra Thong, Baba Ecolodge's 27 wooden pads are about as far off the grid as you can get.
babaecolodge.com

AKATSUKI
Koh Samui
A sequestered stay on the island's west coast, the six-bedroom retreat, designed by Tokyo-based Riccardo Tossani Architecture, is a coherent blend of Thai and Japanese design.
akatsuki-samui.com

GARRYA TONGSAI BAY SAMUI
Koh Samui
Wrapped tightly around a generous private bay, this beachfront resort is scattered with quiet "contemplation pockets" to encourage immersion in nature and create a sense of serenity.
garrya.com

SIX SENSES
Koh Yao Noi
The 56 villas are cocooned in the shade of trees from the former rubber plantation and decked out with private pools, sunken bathtubs and alfresco dining areas that celebrate the surrounding nature.
sixsenses.com

THE SANCTUARY
Koh Phangan
At this hidden refuge guests will discover a restorative combination of healthy smoothies, spa therapies, yoga sessions and detox programmes designed to enrich and revitalise.
thesanctuarythailand.com

PIMALAI RESORT & SPA
Koh Lanta
This 40-hectare tropical plot was acquired back when there were no roads or electricity supply, and the traditional villas have since been seamlessly integrated into the sloping terrain.
pimalai.com

CASTAWAY
Koh Lipe
There's a classic easygoing spirit here. The accommodation is made up of sophisticated darkwood bungalows topped with thatched roofs and positioned on foundational stilts that keep you cool in the island's heat.
kohlipe.castaway-resorts.com

KOYAO BAY PAVILIONS
Koh Yao Noi
Found on Koh Yao Noi's isthmus, the hotel's 18 villas and studios, some with private pools, celebrate seclusion with beaches to swim at that are never further than a short, easy stroll away.
koyaobay.com

THE SAROJIN
Khao Lak
This tropical idyll has found decades-long success in facilitating the slow life. Its premium wellness offering includes body scrubs and facials. We recommend booking the Garden Residence.
sarojin.com

FOOD & DRINK

VIKASA LIFE CAFÉ
Koh Samui
One of the island's leading health-conscious cafés, Vikasa spoils its customers with a fresh and nutritious menu and a food philosophy that champions balance and purity.
vikasa.com

HOUSE OF SUZY
Koh Samui
Drenched in deep burgundy tones and soft lighting, House of Suzy is a low-key cocktail bar that serves up handmade dim sum and reinvented classic drinks.
houseofsuzylamai.com

COCO TAM'S
Koh Samui
This beach bar's rustic setting draws in a relaxed crowd with its palm-thatched roof, dazzling fire show and front-row seats to the island's enchanting sunsets.
62 Tambon Bo Put

TREE TOPS SIGNATURE DINING
Koh Samui
Among the branches of a 120-year-old tree, this gourmet restaurant offers a unique perspective of Koh Samui as the only treetop restaurant on the island.
treetopsrestaurantsamui.com

ROSSINI ICE CREAM
Koh Samui
Rossini Ice Cream has been keeping Koh Samui's residents cool since 1992. More than 50 varieties – both timeless classics and new creations – will please every palate.
rossiniicecream.com

SPICE
Koh Phangan
A candle-lit enclave serving sumptuous seafood, salads and cocktails. The restaurant's owner serves fresh catches from Haad Tien bay.
spicekohphangan.com

LONG DTAI
Koh Samui
The menu at Michelin-starred chef David Thompson's restaurant showcases authentic southern Thai dishes that make use of regional culinary techniques.
longdtai.com

MARIA SEAVIEW RESTAURANT
Koh Panyee
Locally run and complete with a Halal-certified menu, dining here is as much about the experience as the food – a glimpse into everyday life in one of Thailand's most unique communities.
Maria Seaview Restaurant, Village 2, 127/3

SHOP

SPROUT
Koh Phangan
Stocking hand-poured coconut wax candles and plant-based skincare products, this relaxed lifestyle shop allows visitors to dial into the rhythms, flavours, scents and textures of Koh Phangan.
sproutthailand.com

MAKALULU BY ATMAN
Koh Phangan
With an inventory that captures the essence of island living, this chic clothing shop treats its guests to a wardrobe that's all about sustainability, local craftsmanship and thoughtful design.
74/16, Village 1, Thongsala

MAY & CO
Koh Tao
May & Co's shelves are lined with handmade goods: revitalising skincare, high-quality stationery and products from its sustainable Plas-Tao line, which repurposes plastic waste into items such as jewellery and coasters.
Village 1, 9/275

SAMUI HEALTH SHOP
Koh Samui
Samui Health Shop encourages its customers to stock their pantries and bathroom cupboards with a tempting array of natural and organic products.
samuihealthshop.com

FAIR ARTISAN
Koh Samui
Situated in Lamai, Fair Artisan offers a considered selection of jewellery, clothing and homeware, with a particular emphasis on sustainability and local craft. Make sure to leave room in your bag for one of the hand-poured candles.
168 Lamai

ASIA BOOKS
Koh Samui
As Thailand's first and largest English-language book retailer and distributor, Asia Books attracts bibliophiles from all over the world. We recommend visiting the branch at Koh Samui's open-air airport.
asiabooks.com

CENTRAL KRABI
Krabi
This mixed-use development comprises a shopping centre with more than 300 labels, a hotel, residencies and plenty of breezy open-air spaces.
central.co.th

DO

SOUL FRIEND & SPIRITUAL GARDEN
Khao Lak
Born from a passion for mental health, Soul Friend & Spiritual Garden stands out as Khao Lak's only bookstore and the first new-age meditation studio on the southern coast.
soulfriendworld.com

HOUSE OF LUCIE
Koh Samui
This distinct cobalt-blue building displays the work of award-winning photographers from around the world, houses the Koh Samui Art Center, and hosts exhibitions and lectures.
houseoflucie.org

WHERE TO STAY

The Sukhothai 15
bangkok.sukhothai.com

Rosewood 16, 45
rosewoodhotels.com

Public House 16
publichouse-hotels.com

Mandarin Oriental 17
mandarinoriental.com

Na Tanao 1969 18
natanao1969.com

The Siam 18
thesiamhotel.com

Capella Bangkok 19
capellahotels.com

Grand Hyatt Erawan Bangkok 19
hyatt.com

Baan Pomphet 20
baanpomphet.com

Z9 Resort 21
z9resorts.com

The Barai 22
thebarai.com

Chiva-Som 23
chivasom.com

The Standard 23
standardhotels.com

137 Pillars 24
137pillarshotels.com

Raya Heritage 25
rayaheritage.com

Tamarind Village 26
tamarindvillage.com

Tatvani Estate 26
tatvani.com

Ad Lib 27
adlibhotels.co

Sala 28
salahospitality.com

Mason 29
masonpattaya.com

Andaz Hotel 29
hyatt.com

The Dewa Koh Chang 30
thedewakohchang.com

The Retreat 31
theretreatkohchang.com

Paradee 32
paradeethesixthheaven.com

Koh Munnork Private Island 33
munnorkprivateisland.com

Rayavadee Resort 34
rayavadee.com

The Sarojin 34
sarojin.com

Devasom Khao Lak 35
devasom.com

Garrya Tongsai Bay Samui 36
garrya.com

Castaway 37
kohlipe.castaway-resorts.com

The Sanctuary 38
thesanctuarythailand.com

Akatsuki 39
theluxenomad.com

Kamalaya 40
kamalaya.com

Koyao Bay Pavilions 41
koyaobay.com

Pimalai Resort & Spa 41
pimalai.com

Six Senses 42
sixsenses.com

Amanpuri 43
aman.com

Trisara 44
trisara.com

The Naka Phuket 44
thenakaphuket.com

DRINKING & DINING

Bo.lan 49
bolan.co.th

Charmkrung 50
+66 97 994 5523

Gaggan 50
gaggan.com

Potong 51
restaurantpotong.com

Thipsamai 52
thipsamai.com

Appia 53
appia-bangkok.com

Baan Dusit Thani 54
baandusitthani.com

Baan Trok Tua Ngork 54
baantrok.com

Curvy Dining 55
+66 65 989 9242

The Artisans 56
theartisansayutthaya.com

Rorsor127 57
rorsor127.com

Baan Ta Nid 57
+66 81 835 0660

Kamsla 58
23/3 Village 4 Soi Wat Chang Kheng

Praça 59
standardhotels.com

Blackitch Artisan Kitchen 60
blackitch.com

The House by Ginger 60
thehousebygingercm.com

Another Smith 61
+66 64 424 4647

Locus Native Food Lab 62
locusnativefoodlab.com

Kaen 63
+66 83 912 8659

Ma Long Der 63
+66 95 229 5359

Mok 64
+66 95 292 4622

Khao Kwan 65
+66 81 940 0649

Tree Tops Signature Dining 66
treetopsrestaurantsamui.com

Maria Seaview Restaurant 67
+66 99 132 1160

Blue Elephant 68
blueelephant.com

Samut 69
samutphuket.com

Tu Kab Khao 70
+66 76 608 888

Yellow Lane 71
+66 65 123 8378

Harudot 72
nanacoffeeroasters.com

Khagee 73
+66 82 975 7774

Cap 74
+66 85 499 6266

The Gardener 74
+66 65 615 5162

Easterly 75
+66 94 549 5926

Karo 76
+66 61 858 9191

Roots 76
rootsbkk.com

Citizen Tea Canteen 77
+66 95 119 6592

Sangkaew 78
+66 99 367 8439

Sawanbondin Tea House
& Experience 79
+66 81 205 3554

Freaking Out the Neighbourhood 82
freakingout.co

The Norm 82
+66 65 491 4699

Tep Bar 83
+66 98 467 2944

Rusty-Social Club 83
+66 83 620 8939

House of Suzy 84
houseofsuzylamai.com

Coco Tam's 85
+66 91 915 5664

Alone Together 86
sugarraygroup.com

Smalls 86
+66 89 666 5429

Kad Kokoa 87
kadkokoa.co

Kanvela 87
kanvelachocolate.com

Rocket Ice Cream 88
+66 81 723 3600

Torry's 89
torrys.com

Ba Hao Tian Mi 89
+66 97 995 4543

The Distillery Phuket 90
thedistilleryphuket.com

Granmonte Estate 91
granmonte.com

DESIGN & RETAIL

The Decorum 95
thedecorumbkk.com

JBB 96
jbbmenswear.com

Asava 97
asavagroup.com

Vvon Sugunnasil 97
vvonsugunnasil.com

Long Goy 98
+66 89 850 5334

Palit 98
palitpalit.myshopify.com

ES Phuket 99
+66 89 924 9429

Paint Palette 99
+66 89 362 9669

Warehouse 30 100
warehouse30.com

Pana Objects 100
pana-objects.com

Wit's Collection 101
+66 53 023 809

Akaliko 102
akalikodesignshop.com

Sprout 103
sprouthailand.com

Container 104
containerbag.net

Chabatree 104
chabatree.com

Pañpuri 105
panpuri.com

Eastern Glass 106
+66 92 240 4141

Korakot 107
korakotaromdee.com

Vila Cini 108
vilacini.com

Sop Moei Arts 108
sopmoeiarts.com

Doy Din Dang Pottery 109
+66 61 093 3131

Earth & Fire Ceramics 110—111
+66 82 565 5971

Don Moo Din 112
+66 89 128 7390

Nakamol 113
nakamolthailand.com

Emquartier 114
emquartier.co.th

Siam Paragon 115
siamparagon.co.th

Chatuchak Weekend Market 116
chatuchakmarket.org

Jing Jai Market 117
jingjaicentralchiangmai.com

CULTURE

Museum of Contemporary Art 129
mocabangkok.com

Bangkok Kunsthalle 130
khaoyaiart.com

Chiang Rai Contemporary Art
Museum 131
+66 88 418 5431

Maiiam 132
maiiam.com

Molam Bus 132
jimthompsonfarm.com

Khao Yai Art Forest 133
khaoyaiart.com

Numthong Art Space 134
numthongartspace.com

Dharma Park and Inson Wongsam
Art Gallery 135
inson-wongsam.com

Bangkok Art & Culture Centre 136
bacc.or.th

Thailand Creative & Design
Center 136
tcdc.or.th

Kalm Village 137
kalmvillage.com

Jim Thompson Art Center 140
jimthompsonartcenter.org

The Queen Sirikit Museum
of Textiles 141
qsmtthailand.org

Thai Film Archive 141
fapot.or.th

Baan Dam Museum 142
+66 53 776 333

Open House 143
centralembassy.com

The Booksmith 144
thebooksmith.co.th

Asia Books 144
asiabooks.com

Soul Friend & Spiritual Garden 145
soulfriendworld.com

Zudrangma Records 146
zudrangmarecords.com

Embassy Diplomat Screens 147
embassycineplex.com

Rajadamnern Stadium 148
rajadamnern.com

Araksa Tea Garden 149
araksatea.com

PUT DOWN ROOTS

Onion 192
onion.co.th

Bodinchapa Architects 193
bodinchapa.com

Sher Maker Studio 193
shermaker.com

PDM Brand 194
pdmbrand.com

Studio Freehand 195
studio-freehand.com

Chanintr Craft 196
chanintr.com

Alexander Lamont 197
alexanderlamont.com

Moonler 197
moonler.com

Foreign Correspondents' Club
of Thailand 198
fccthai.com

The Commons 199
thecommonsbkk.com

ACKNOWLEDGEMENTS

MONOCLE

Editorial Director & Chairman
Tyler Brûlé

Editor in Chief
Andrew Tuck

Creative Director
Richard Spencer Powell

Production Director
Jacqueline Deacon

Chief Sub Editor
Yo Zushi

Photography Director
Matthew Beaman

Art Director
Sam Brogan

MONOCLE BOOKS

Head of Book Publishing
Virginia McLeod

Deputy Editor
Josh Lee

Assistant Editor
Aimee Dexter

Photography Editor
Sara Taglioretti

Production Coordinator
Marta Fernàndez Canut

THAILAND: THE MONOCLE HANDBOOK

Editor
James Chambers

Deputy Editor
Aimee Dexter

Designer
Carey Alborough

Photography Editor
Sara Taglioretti

Sub Editor
Matt Dupuy

Production Coordinator
Marta Fernàndez Canut

PRINCIPAL WRITERS
James Chambers
Aimee Dexter
Rory Jones
Virginia McLeod

WRITERS
Gary Boyle
Uracha Chaiyapinunt
Niki Chatikavanij
Joe Cummings
Claudia Jacob
Julia Jenne
Joseph Koh
Josh Lee
Millie McArthur
Lucrezia Motta
Tom Vater

RESEARCHER
Hikari Hida

PRINCIPAL PHOTOGRAPHER
Natthawut Taeja

PHOTOGRAPHERS
John Clewley
Sven Ellsworth
Foto Momo
Chakrawooth Kaewjunthong
Duangsuda Kittivattananon
Fred Lahache
Jonathan Leijonhufvud
Andrew Loiterton
Virginia McLeod
Benjamin McMahon
Fiona Ohanlon
Kiattipong Panchee
Joe Perri
PanoramicStudio
Owen Raggett
Adisorn Ruangsiridecha

Max Sangkaew
Pichan Sujritsatit
Kobkit Thitithanawat
Wison Tungthhunya
Nicolas Voisin
Christopher Wise
Thanik Yindeepit

ILLUSTRATORS
Owen Gatley
Matteo Riva
Nikolai Senin & Natalia Senina

IMAGE LIBRARIES
Alamy
Getty Images
Shutterstock

ADVISORY BOARD
Jirawat "Bote" Benchakarn
Kanachai "Kit" Bencharongkul
Siradej "Champ" Donavanik
Kamolthip "Kim" Kimaree
Wathunyu "Jay" Pikulsawad
Sirapol "Guy" Ridhiprasart
Gwen Robinson
David Schafer
Vorravit "Pui" Siripark
Chanintr Sirisant
Belle Sirisant
Shane Suvikapakornkul
Vicharee Vichit-Vadakan
Gavin Vongkusolkit
Nick Wattanavekin
Chomwan Weeraworawit

SPECIAL THANKS
Alexandra Aldea
Virgiliu Andone
Vanessa Bird
Chloé Lake
Blake Matich
Alex Milnes
Waranya Panruksa
Pan Siripark
Panvadee Uraisin
Adam Workman
Sonia Zhuravlyova
Yo Zushi

Join our club

In 2007, Monocle was launched as a monthly magazine briefing on global affairs, business, design and more. Today we have a thriving print business, a radio station, shops, cafés, books, films and events. At our core is the simple belief that there will always be a place for a brand that is committed to telling fresh stories, delivering good journalism and being on the ground around the world. We're Zürich and London-based and have bureaux in Hong Kong, Paris and Tokyo. Subscribe at *monocle.com*.

Monocle Magazine

Monocle is published 10 times a year, including two double issues (July/August and December/January). We also have annual specials: *Design Directory*, *The Escapist* and *The Entrepreneurs*. Look out for our seasonal newspapers too.

Monocle Radio

Our round-the-clock online radio station delivers global news and shows covering foreign affairs, urbanism, business, culture, food and drink, design and print media. You can listen live or download shows from *monocle.com/radio* – or wherever you get your podcasts.

Books

Since 2013, Monocle has been publishing books such as this one, covering a range of topics from home design to how to live a gentler life. Also available in this series are *Handbook*s for Portugal, Spain, France, Greece and Switzerland. All our books are available on our website, through our distributor, Thames & Hudson, and at all good bookshops.

Monocle Minute

Monocle's smartly appointed family of newsletters comes from our team of editors and correspondents around the world. From the daily *Monocle Minute* to *The Monocle Weekend Editions* and our weekly *Monocle On Design* special, sign up to get the latest in affairs, entrepreneurship and design, straight to your inbox every day – all for free. *monocle.com/minute*

MONOCLE